ITALIAN
Style

ITALIAN
Style

Jane Gordon-Clark

PHOTOGRAPHS
Simon Upton

ADAMS MEDIA CORPORATION
Holbrook, Massachusetts

To Charlotte, Venetia, Fenella,
Sam, and Matthew,
with whom I have shared many
of the pleasures of Italy.

Copyright © Frances Lincoln Limited 1999
Text copyright © Jane Gordon-Clark 1999
Photographs by Simon Upton, copyright © Simon Upton 1999,
except those listed on page 144

First published in the United States by
Adams Media Corporation
260 Center Street
Holbrook, MA 02343

ITALIAN STYLE was edited, designed
and produced by Frances Lincoln Limited
4 Torriano Mews, Torriano Avenue
London NW5 2RZ

ISBN 1-58062-103-1

Typeset by Frances Lincoln Limited

Printed in Singapore

9 8 7 6 5 4 3 2 1

CIP information available upon request
from the publisher

PAGE 1 This mellow stone *loggia* in a restored farmhouse offers shelter
from the strong Tuscan sun. The basket hanging from a decorative
metal hook on the wall is used during the olive harvest.

PAGES 2–3 Few people strip back their walls in the process of
restoration and find a delicate fresco underneath. In this bedroom a
faint border design has been revealed, which is interesting enough
to define the style of the room but not to dominate it.

THIS PAGE Some of the wildflowers that grow in the rolling meadows
of the Italian countryside in the spring and early summer have been
gathered to make a posy, filling a simple white pitcher.

Contents

PREFACE

Why ask an Englishwoman to write a book on Italian Style? I think this is a reasonable question—for who knows more about a country than its own inhabitants? But being at the heart of a subject makes it harder to take an overview, to distinguish the fundamental elements from the confusing details. In a country whose visual style is like a tapestry, intricately woven with different strands, it sometimes helps to have the distance to see the overall design rather than the individual threads.

Entire libraries have been given over to the cultural history of Italy and the impact of its visual arts. From ancient Rome to the Renaissance, Italian artists and philosophers have changed the way that other Europeans look at the world. This history and visual inheritance is reflected in Italian interiors today, not only in the magnificent architectural style of country villas and urban palazzi, but also in those simpler houses whose fabric is so closely related to the land from which it was made.

Most people know something of Italy's history as separate city states and regions until unification, and they may have more than a passing acquaintance with the great artists of the Renaissance, the Baroque, the Rococo, and beyond. But to put it all into perspective, I have started the book with a short cultural history, followed by a swift tour of the main regions of Italy, which differ from each other so much that they could be separate countries.

The eye of a designer is different from that of an art historian. It can pick out those aspects that show most closely the underlying structure—the proportion, symmetry, and balance—which are fundamental to Italian style, but are sometimes obscured by the richness of the decoration and the accumulated possessions of succeeding generations. The rooms illustrated in Italian Style *have been chosen to show this structure. Looking at historic interiors with a contemporary eye also enables me to show rooms that have a resonance with modern interior design. These are all houses that are meant to be enjoyed by their owners, rather than svelte urban apartments designed for maximum ease of living and work.*

When I was 12, my father took the family on a kind of Grand Tour, which included the Italian Riviera, Florence, Siena, and Rome. The sights and sounds of Italy, the smells, the heat, the strange tastes, the paintings, the buildings, and the buzzing Lambrettas, made an indelible impression on my young mind, and started a passion for all things Italian. As a student I absorbed as much about Italian architecture and art by observing and drawing as by reading and writing. Perhaps a love affair with Italy clouds the vision to those things that are less than perfect, but no matter. In reply to the original question, there can be no-one better to celebrate the essence of Italian style than a woman who loves it. Italians understand all about that!

OPPOSITE A Romantic, imaginary landscape, painted in the late 18th century, appears to be framed by the swagged valance above and border decoration below. Similar paintings decorate the other three walls, sweeping the viewer into the realms of an idealized Arcadia.

ITALIAN BACKGROUNDS

Italy is filled with glorious architecture and historic interiors that provide an ever-present reminder of a complex and varied past. This immensely rich cultural heritage—the balance and symmetry of Roman architecture, the magnificence of Renaissance decoration, and the flamboyance of the Baroque— provides signposts to the evolution of Italian style. An equally important influence, however, is the land itself, which varies enormously from north to south, east to west, and can determine the homes that people live in, and the colors that they choose to reflect their surroundings.

The panel decorations in the window recesses opposite are based on the style of painting used by Raphael in the Vatican *loggia*. His ideas were inspired by the then-recently discovered remains of an ancient palace belonging to the Roman Emperor Augustus.

HISTORICAL INFLUENCES

One of the earliest cultures in Italy was that of the Etruscans, who had strong trade links with Greece and imported large quantities of pottery and statuary. The vast majority of surviving Etruscan artifacts have been found in tombs and include fine metalwork and carved sarcophagi. In some ancient towns, such as Perugia in Umbria, there are networks of Etruscan tombs lying beneath the medieval streets and buildings, which local people still use as short cuts.

The Romans obliterated most of the earlier Etruscan culture to make room for their own buildings, which are evident all over Italy. Even today in some cities, classical remains provide a backdrop to everyday life. Ancient walls form part of later buildings and massive constructions, such as the Colosseum and the Baths of Caracalla in Rome, stand as reminders of an empire that at its height stretched from Britain across western and southern Europe to Mesopotamia and the Caspian Sea.

During the Middle Ages distinct regional styles emerged. Those cities that had strong trade links with the Orient developed exotic architecture that was clearly inspired by Byzantium, of which the bulbous domes and glittering mosaics of St. Mark's Cathedral in

Venice are a renowned example. This was later integrated with the northern gothic style to produce structures such as the whimsical Doge's Palace in St. Mark's Square. A purer form of Gothic is found farther north in Milan Cathedral, whose façade is a light and airy confection of pointed arches, crockets, pinnacles, and spires. It is a style of architecture that resulted from the close links between the courts of northern Italy and those in France and Bohemia. In central Italy, gothic buildings in Florence, Siena, and Assisi share a more robust architectural vocabulary; while in southern Italy and Sicily, there is a mix of Greek, Roman, byzantine, Moorish, and Norman styles that reflects the succession of invaders and colonizers.

By the beginning of the 15th century, the new spirit of the Renaissance was asserting itself in Florence. Scholars, patrons, and artists began to re-evaluate classical texts and ideas, while elsewhere others were uncovering buildings that dated back to the ancient Roman Empire. This heralded a new awareness of classical architectural concepts as a source of inspiration.

The Florentine architect Filippo Brunelleschi (1377–1446), whose most famous achievement was to span the vast dome of Florence Cathedral, made careful studies of the antique buildings in Rome and adhered to the concepts of proportion and balance they embodied in the plans and elevations of his own work. He copied, too, the arches, columns, capitals, pediments, architraves, and other architectural details employed by the Romans to embellish their structures. Together with his fellow architect and humanist, Leon Battista Alberti (1404–72), whose buildings also emulated the ancient Roman ideal, his influence on succeeding generations was profound, not just in Italy but throughout Europe and the reach of Western civilization.

THIS PAGE AND OPPOSITE The simplicity of many Etruscan and Roman artifacts has withstood the test of time; indeed, some styles are still in production. Statues of emperors, gods, and goddesses peep from beneath bridges and dominate gardens, often displayed alongside the Christian figures that replaced them. Later developments, such as gothic and byzantine styles, can also be seen many years after the trade links that brought them to Italy's shores have disappeared.

Despite the gothic shape of this arch at Torre di Bellosguardo, the garden scene of plants and birds has a clear affinity with ancient Roman wall painting. Not only does it use many of the colors found decorating the walls of Roman villas, but also the way that the subjects are drawn is very similar. In this fresco, stylized orange and lemon trees alternate in successive arches against a fiery red background. Birds can be seen in and above the trees, and below among the honesty leaves. The scene is bounded by a *trompe-l'oeil* fence.

During the Renaissance the conceptual divisions between architect, painter, designer, and decorator, which are now clearly delineated, were not of particular significance. Raphael (1483–1520), for example, not only was a painter, but also studied the construction of ancient Roman buildings and was commissioned to work as architect with his contemporary Donato Bramante on the Vatican. He was therefore involved in the planning of a building, the Stanza della Segnatura, for which he later painted a magnificent series of frescoes. Here his subjects married the complex relationship between classical learning and Christian belief, which underpinned the intellectual thought of the Renaissance and provided a source of inspiration for hundreds of later artists.

Raphael's interest in ancient Roman decoration affected his approach not only to the architectural structure of a building, but also to its interior embellishment. When he was commissioned to decorate the Vatican *loggia*, he explored the newly unearthed Roman buildings and found decorations on the walls that had lain undisturbed for more than a thousand years. The excitement of discovery must have been immense as he was lowered in a basket tied by a rope through holes in the ceiling and glimpsed, in the flickering light of a candle, the rich colors and highly decorated frescoes of ancient Rome. He copied what he saw there, reproducing the swirling acanthus leaves, the arabesques, the panel designs, and the grotesques. (The use of the term "grotesque" to describe a Roman-style form of decoration is derived from the Italian word *grotta* and refers to the buried rooms in which these designs were found.) Raphael's work in the Vatican was widely copied and strongly influenced the stylistic development of decorative embellishment throughout Europe. Even today designers of fabrics and wallpapers consciously or unconsciously incorporate motifs inspired by Raphael's designs.

The Italian passion for *trompe-l'oeil* painting as a form of interior decoration also had its origins in ancient Rome. In the house of Livia and Augustus on the Palatine Hill, for example, rooms were painted with three-dimensional architectural decoration, which brought the illusion of depth and space to a small area. Renaissance painters took this art of playing tricks with space and reality into new realms, producing *trompe-l'oeil* columns and pilasters that appeared to support the ceiling, frescoes that were made to look like carved stone, classical figures that seemed to hold up heavy pediments over doorways, and painted landscapes that pierced the walls like windows. Walls were sometimes divided into panels and painted with lifelike festoons of flowers, garlands of leaves and fruit, and colorful swirling arabesques that united to create an intricate and lavish decoration.

One of the earliest painters to perfect *trompe-l'oeil* was Andrea Mantegna (*c.*1431–1506). His decorations in the palace of the Duke of Mantua include an intriguing *sotto in sù* ceiling, painted as if there was a hole in the roof, through which the viewer can see the sky and a crowd of people looking down. This idea began an enthusiastic exploration into the possibilities of *trompe-l'oeil* by many other painters in Italy, including Paolo Veronese (*c.*1528–88) who decorated the walls of the Villa Barbaro at Maser. In this *trompe-l'oeil*, life-sized figures surprise the viewer by appearing through a half-open door; at the end of a corridor a hunter comes in carrying a dead rabbit; and above the spectator a group of people—the mistress of the house and her servants—look inquiringly over a painted balcony.

By the beginning of the 17th century, the grandiose ideas of the Baroque were beginning to emerge. Although the architectural and decorative vocabulary still stemmed from the antique, it was interpreted in a far more fluid way. Frescoes and decorative painting had amazing vitality, and every inch of wall and ceiling space was covered with painting of astounding exuberance. The concepts were grandiose and theatrical. A strong color palette and deep *chiaroscuro* (the balance of light and shade in a picture) took inspiration from the artist Michelangelo Merisi da Caravaggio (1573–1610), whose technique of throwing points of light into areas of high drama made the work look as if it was lit by spotlights, creating the excitement of participation.

In Rome, papal patronage led to an explosion of the Baroque architectural vocabulary in churches designed by the two masters of the style: Gianlorenzo Bernini (1598–1680) and Francesco Borromini (1599–1667). Both were sculptors as well as architects, and their work embraces a creative vigor and fluidity of form far beyond the calm restraints of pure classicism. Borromini's design for one of his early works, San Carlo alle Quattro Fontane, displays a rhythmic deployment of mass and space combined with a skillful interplay of curved lines that at the time was considered innovative and daring. Bernini's buildings, sculptures, and tombs have left an indelible mark on Rome. One of his most famous public works is the fountain in Piazza Navona, which captures four massively hewn figures as they cast the gift of water to the four corners of the earth.

The Baroque era was characterized by exuberant decoration, such as this early 18th-century fresco by Fontebasso, which fills the space between the cornice and the ceiling of a bedroom wall. The two figures seem to be lit from below, as if they are acting on a stage. To their right, a dog looks on with a quizzical expression.

In the 18th century, the heavy drama and passion of the Baroque was replaced by the lighter palette of the Rococo. Furniture became more delicate, with swirls, twirls, and elaborately painted decoration. Sometimes découpage techniques were used on inexpensive wooden pieces to give pictorial embellishment. The walls of villas and *palazzi* were often decorated with free-flowing stucco work, and pale, bright colors were fashionable.

The work of Venetian artist Giovanni Battista Tiepolo (1696–1770) represents the purest expression of the Rococo in Italy with his gigantic wall and ceiling paintings in which dramatic illusions almost overwhelm the viewer. Horse-drawn chariots spring from wispy clouds overhead while chubby putti cavort about an endless receding sky. The walls are painted with scenes of such realism that they draw the viewer in to participate in the action.

Just as the decorative style of the Renaissance was deeply influenced by the ancient Roman discoveries, so that of the 18th century was dominated by the remarkable finds at Pompeii and Herculaneum. When Mount Vesuvius erupted in A.D. 79, volcanic ash completely obliterated the two cities, and they stayed covered until 18th-century archeologists began to dig among the ruins. Magnificent pots decorated with athletes were found in tombs, and cooking utensils and objects of everyday living were unearthed. As the exciting excavations continued, whole rooms with wonderfully rich decorations on the walls came to see the light of day again after their lengthy entrapment.

The excitement of the discoveries stimulated a whole new interest in the classical antique, not just in Italy, but all over Europe. Architects and artists made visits to Pompeii and returned with sketchbooks full of classical motifs and decorations that they incorporated into their designs. The discoveries in Pompeii, and the reawakened interest in ancient Rome, led to the development of the neoclassical movement. This style was favored for public building where its restrained adherence to the pure forms of classical antiquity were considered more appropriate than the excesses of the Rococo and Baroque.

The neoclassical movement reinterpreted the underlying themes of balance, proportion, and decorative ornament that inform Italian style. Of course, it was followed by other movements, which drew on the same principles to a greater or lesser extent to channel artists in new and exciting directions. Even today, designers and architects acknowledge these historical influences, with their extraordinary range of visual reference and diversity, although their work, which is renowned for its experimental modernism, often seems the antithesis of classical form and structure.

ABOVE Rococo curves and flourishes in molded stucco are formed in panels decorating the walls on each side of the fireplace and its ornate overmantel. The almond green and dusty pink are characteristic of the softer, more delicate colors favored during the 18th century.

OPPOSITE The birth of the neoclassical movement was seen as a return to sobriety and restraint. An example of the new decoration can be seen on these door panels, which open onto a corridor. The backs of the doors are flat and are painted with rustic scenes by Ignazio Moder. This Tyrolean painter spent nine months in 1780 decorating the corridor with a continuous fresco that was inspired by the work of Bartolomeo Zocci (see page 53).

REGIONAL INFLUENCES

Italy is a spectacularly beautiful country with enormous variations in landscape and climate. Before unification in 1861, it was made up of a series of independent city states, kingdoms, and papal lands, each with their own cultural inheritance, dialect, and economic history. Geography and climate also played an important part in defining the unique character and style of each region. A journey from the north of Italy, down through the center to the southern-most tip of the toe and across the sea to Sicily, takes travelers through an immense variety of scenery and introduces them to a wealth of colors, architectural styles, decorative elements, and ways of life.

Crowning the north of the country like a glittering tiara, and separating her from the rest of Europe, are the Alps, the highest mountain range in the continent, which mark the Italian borders with France, Switzerland, and Austria. These adjacent countries have a very strong influence in the region. Traditional houses look like alpine chalets with their stone walls and heavy use of wooden siding. Austrian styles are particularly prevalent in the Dolomites, reflecting the fact that this area was part of the Hapsburg Empire until 1919. Tyrolean houses are built in wood with deeply overhanging eves, fretwork balconies, and decorative shutters. Inside the atmosphere is cozy with large open fires and comfortable furniture. The walls are often paneled with wood, and the locally made furniture is decorated with traditional hand-painted motifs. Just as outside the clear blue sky provides a dramatic contrast to the glistening white mountain snow and the rich dark green of the trees, so inside the decoration is in primary greens, blues, reds, and yellows, all with a background of natural wood. There is plenty of bright white, too, in the bed linen and the thick, locally made lace. These pretty houses were originally built as farms, but they are now mainly the cherished second homes of enthusiastic skiers and mountain lovers.

At the base of the mountains the retreating glaciers of the Ice Age created a spectacular lake district. Snowcapped mountains provide a setting of breathtaking splendor for the shimmering lakes and vast forests. This visual dynamic of the rugged landscape juxtaposed with wide expanses of calm water has for centuries lured visitors in need of relaxation. For hundreds of years people have enjoyed the elegance and style that is unique to this part of Italy. Pliny was born here, at Novum Comum, and the English Romantic poets Percy Bysshe Shelley and William Wordsworth frequented the dramatic shores of Lake Como.

This map dates from the late 18th century, and so shows the fabric of Italy before unification in 1861. Each of the various regions had its own customs and styles, which were a product of many factors including landscape and climate. Although it is well over 100 years since the country was divided, most Italians still identify with their native area, describing themselves, for example, as Sicilian or Tuscan, or more specifically as Venetian or Roman.

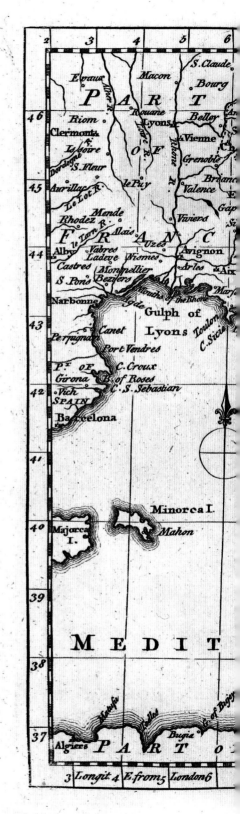

Elegant 18th- and 19th-century villas in a variety of styles line the lakeside, and are punctuated by renaissance villas and modern buildings that are constructed in a traditional style. The interiors are created to be as cool as possible with marble floors and large windows. Many of the villas are surrounded by formal gardens of balustraded terraces and box hedges. The strong Spanish influence in this area is revealed by magnificent gates and interior furnishings made from wrought iron.

Farther down, on the Adriatic coast, Venice is a unique city filled with spectacular architecture and interiors that are more ostentatious and ornate than any of her rivals. The city's initial prosperity was from salt drawn from the lagoon, but real wealth came through trade with the East. During the Crusades, Venetian ships carried armies to their wars and then returned loaded with exotic goods. At Constantinople, a great bazaar that attracted traders from around the globe, Venetian merchants could purchase furs from Siberia, amber from the Baltic, and carpets, ivories, silks, and spices from India, Tibet, and China. They also picked up exotic ideas for the architecture of their buildings, and today a gentle glide along the Grand Canal reveals a magnificent variety of highly decorated façades with a clear Moorish influence, culminating in the Doge's Palace in St. Mark's Square. To this architectural exuberance were added grand *palazzi*, displaying the magnificence of baroque taste and classicism combined with the later refinements of 18th-century Europe. Today, the painted stucco façades pass by in a harmony of rose-tinted colors—from deep rich russet, crimson, crushed loganberry, and plum, to corals, terracottas, and the palest petal creamy pink—that is broken occasionally by a splash of yellow, ocher, or green.

Venetian *palazzi* were clearly designed as merchants' palaces, whatever contrary message may be conveyed by their exotic exteriors. The entrance on the ground floor was via the canal and had doors large enough to accept big cargo. This was unloaded into

the shady warehouse rooms that were also on the ground floor. The merchant lived "above the store" on the light, spacious *piano nobile* (main floor). No expense was spared decorating the upstairs rooms with astounding feats of the plasterer's art; three-dimensional putti disporting among flowers and swags of pretend silk; great wooden beams painted with intricate patterns and dazzlingly gilded; or superb frescoes, perhaps by that great 18th-century Venetian master of the technique, Tiepolo (see page 16). The walls were often hung with heavy silk damask, or painted with *trompe-l'oeil* to give the illusion of inlaid marble. Sometimes they were divided into decorative panels and painted in colors that seem almost gaudy to the modern eye. The floors, not to be outdone by all this richness, were frequently inlaid with vibrantly colored marble or made from terrazzo that sparkled with semi-precious stones.

When the city became too hot and pungent, richer Venetians escaped to their farms in the cooler Veneto region, just outside Venice. Many of them would decamp for the entire summer, taking with them not just their servants, but their furniture and household goods as well. Some of the most beautiful villas in the Veneto region were built as farmhouses by the classical architect Andrea Palladio (1508–80), whose *Quattro libri dell'architettura* (1570) has influenced generations of architects. These are no ordinary farmhouses, but imposing country villas of exquisite proportion and balance with symmetrical ground plans, evenly spaced façades, and centrally placed porticos. Typical are the Villa Malcontenta on the Brenta Canal and the Villa Barbaro at Maser, where Paolo Veronese decorated the walls with superb frescoes (see page 15).

OPPOSITE Soaring high above the little town of Allegre, the cliffs of Monte Civetta in the Dolomites provide a spectacular backdrop to the snow-covered lake in the depths of winter.

ABOVE RIGHT The classical proportions of Villa Saraceno in the Veneto region reveal the authorship of the renowned architect, Andrea Palladio.

OVERLEAF After a day transporting visitors on the Grand Canal in Venice, a flight of gondolas has been wrapped up for the evening and tethered to wooden stakes that are firmly bedded in the silt of the canal.

Building in the country allowed more space than was ever possible in Venice, where houses were, of necessity, crammed together. Formal gardens were constructed around the country houses, with low box hedges curving in intricate designs around flowerbeds, avenues of gentle walks through trees, and colonnades of sculptures to divert the eye.

Geographically the heart of Italy, but also the area that to most non-Italians is quintessentially Italian, the countryside of Tuscany and Umbria looks as if it has been plucked straight from the background of a renaissance painting. Travelers may feel a pleasant shock of recognition when they first see the bumpy hills crowned with terracotta villages, the tall cypress trees lining the road to a country villa, and the fortified castles with tall watchtowers cropping up at every distant vantage point.

Florence, the capital of Tuscany and the birthplace of the Renaissance, was the most powerful city in Europe during the 15th century. Banking and trade were the base of her fortunes, and the ruling Medici family the most prosperous bankers in Europe. Financial success on a superlative scale underpinned munificent philanthropy toward artists, architects, writers, musicians, scholars, and poets who flourished under the Medici patronage and that of other successful families. Their names are a roll call of the greatest artists of their time: Donatello, Ghiberti, Fra Filippo Lippi, Fra Angelico, Alberti, Brunelleschi, Ghirlandaio, Botticelli, della Robbia, Uccello, Gozzoli, Pollaiuolo, Vasari, Leonardo da Vinci, and Michelangelo. The Renaissance was an artistic flowering greater than anything the world had known since the ancient Greeks and unsurpassed since. At the end of the century, the religious and political reformer Girolamo Savonarola (1452–98) tried unsuccessfully to put an end to it with his grim exhortations for repentance and massive bonfires of all that was considered licentious or profane.

The imposing *palazzi* that line the streets of Florence are a visible sign of great wealth, yet their somewhat forbidding façades provide a striking contrast with the fanciful style of the Venetians. Florentine architects were working to the strict rules of classical proportion in the design and embellishment of their buildings and sought to perfect the concepts of balance and symmetry they studied in the remains of ancient Rome. They also had to provide protection, for Florence (like many Italian cities) was frequently a hotbed of violence.

THIS PAGE AND OPPOSITE Florence was often under attack during the turbulent Middle Ages, so lookout towers were built on the surrounding hills. Grander houses within the city were also strongly fortified, with massive walls and iron window grilles on the ground floors, although the stark architecture was often softened by statuary and stone ornamentation. Today, a view across the city is dominated by Brunelleschi's famous dome to Florence Cathedral.

The massively hewn stone blocks on the lower floors and heavy iron window grilles give way to a lighter treatment on the upper floors, more spaciously articulated with windows and decorated with classical ornamentation. Likewise, imposing doorways onto the street open out into enclosed courtyards in a layout that is repeated in the *palazzi* of old towns throughout Italy. Today, the grandest of these palaces are museums, but many of the smaller ones are hotels or lived in by descendants of the original owners. Divided up, they make magnificent apartments for all the family, their grand and lofty rooms resonating with history.

In the Tuscan countryside outside Florence, Lorenzo de' Medici (1449–92) built several grand villas with entrances emblazoned with the family crest and elaborate renaissance decoration in all the important rooms. Many other noble families followed his example, giving the area an architectural distinction that has filtered down into less grand country dwellings and farmhouses. As a consequence, even farm buildings display an elegance that is unusual in other rural areas in Italy.

Traveling through the Tuscan and Umbrian countryside can seem like a pilgrimage to the great medieval monasteries and cathedrals built and decorated by artists such as Cimabue, Simone Martini, and Giotto for the greater glory of God. The lovely medieval hill towns of Siena, Cortona, Gubbio, Perugia, Orvieto, Todi, and Assisi were constructed in a way mirrored in smaller towns and villages all over the region. Houses, stores, and churches cluster tightly together, facing each other over cobbled streets so narrow that washing can be strung across and lively conversations fly from one side to the other. Quite unexpectedly, the shady streets open up into a grand *piazza*, a light and spacious area for holding markets, celebrating festivals, or just meeting friends in the daily *passeggiata* or promenade.

These towns are surrounded with massive stone walls for protection, for the Middle Ages were times of extreme violence, when family rivalries erupted into bloodbaths; and guild was pitched against guild, clan against clan, village against village, town against town, and then all formed different factions against a major aggressor. This was the time of ferocious battles between Guelphs and Ghibellines, evidence of which can still be seen in the towers and castles scattered about the towns and countryside. Allegiance to the noble Ghibelline cause was proclaimed in curiously shaped fishtail battlements at the top of the towers, while the Pope's supporters, the Guelphs, built square ones. It is hard to reconcile this extraordinary history of violence with the peaceful rural landscape depicted by Giotto and still seen today.

In the past, farmhouses and rural buildings in Tuscany and Umbria were the equivalent of tied cottages, but in the 1950s far-reaching land reforms meant that thousands of rural dwellings were abandoned as their inhabitants moved to the towns and cities. Gradually, however, people who were in love with the idyllic countryside and the relaxed way of life, and generally in tune with a desire for rural peace, began to see the potential of these buildings and started to buy and restore them. Today, caring owners have returned many of the houses as far as possible to their original state, with the inclusion, of course, of electricity and modern plumbing. Rounded terracotta tiles have been lovingly replaced on roofs, gathering the patina of age, and walls have been reconstructed using limestone, sandstone, and red clay drawn from the local soil, so that the buildings look as if they have grown naturally out of the landscape.

The interiors reflect this simplicity with their natural terracotta floors, unadorned color-washed or plain white walls, wooden beams and shuttered windows. Kitchens are tiled traditionally and simply decorated. The main rooms are furnished in a way that looks spare, but not sparse, with prominence given to practical pieces that are of good quality. The furniture is traditionally dark wood, sometimes new, but in time-honored designs. The overall effect has created a style that has a resonance with the current desire for a natural life, unencumbered with the artifice and sophistication of urban living, to which so many people aspire.

Before it became fashionable among Europeans to have a piece of rural Tuscany as a retreat, the coast proved an unrivaled draw to Italians, and most still choose it as their vacation destination. In the north, the Italian extension of the French Riviera has a rocky shoreline with sheer-sided cliffs stretching into deep valleys inland,

Umbria is known as the green heart of Italy. Its heavily wooded hillsides are filled with oak trees, interspersed with chestnut, birch, hawthorn, and ilex, while occasional lines of cypress trees stand like exclamation points at the side of the white roads. In the spring, the gorse bushes flower, spattering the landscape with vivid splashes of yellow, and later wide-open meadows are filled with wildflowers. During the summer, the hedgerows are heavy with wild roses and honeysuckle, which give way to blackberries in the fall. This is the time of year for mushrooming and harvesting the grapes, before picking olives on frosty November days. Dotted all over the landscape are traditional farmhouses that blend into the landscape with their mellow stone walls and terracotta tiled roofs. Many of them have been converted into comfortable second homes, but strict planning laws have meant that the countryside has retained its timeless quality.

sometimes so thickly wooded and narrow that the sun never penetrates to the bottom. Seaside villas, however grand, have to perch on tiny parcels of land on the steeply terraced hillside; but what they lack in space, they more than make up for in spectacular views and lush subtropical gardens. The larger Ligurian resorts, such as Alassio and San Remo, have long promenades bordered by grand hotels with elegant façades on one side and long sandy beaches on the other. The architecture dates largely from the 19th century, which was when the international élite flocked to these towns. Many of the villas have a whimsical holiday feel. Neoclassical villas sit next to neo-gothic, Moorish next to art nouveau, all festooned with plenty of ornament to liven up the exterior.

A complete contrast in size, fishing villages such as Portofino are quaint, bijou, and seriously fashionable, with harbors where sleek yachts jostle for position. Picturesque village houses rise higgledy-piggledy up the hills above tiny sandy beaches. The walls are painted in colors that make the villages look like jewel boxes from a distance. Raspberry pink, coral, and an infinite spectrum of yellow contrast gaily with pale shades of blue in cobalt, hyacinth, and aquamarine, echoing the transparent sea.

Inside, the decoration is relaxed and cool, with white stucco walls, glazed floor tiles, and comfortable but elegant furniture. The beds may have white gauze hangings to catch the breeze and provide protection from flying insects. The sheets are likely to be made from crisp white linen. Simplicity is the key, so that precious antiques, or carefully chosen pieces of contemporary furniture, are given prominence in uncluttered surroundings.

In Roman times, roads from the ancient capital radiated to every part of the Empire so that, if followed to their source, they did all lead to Rome. Along the coast, the Via Aurelia winds its way from southern France to end in this great city. Buildings in Rome from the time of the Empire to the present day have been constructed to reflect its glory, strength, power, and magnificence. As the center of the Roman Catholic Church, the Vatican City—a tiny enclave within Rome—has drawn a steady flow of artists and scholars to the region, whose masterpieces bear witness to an age of faith. The splendor of Rome, which is apparent when viewed from the streets, is magnified a hundredfold in the interiors, where the Italians' love of display finds its fullest expression.

In southern Italy, the port of Naples is the country's third largest city. Founded by the Greeks in the 6th century B.C., it was an important center in Roman times. During the Middle Ages and beyond, it was a kingdom in its own right, until it fell under Spanish rule. This historical mix is reflected in the architecture of the city—

design in Naples was particularly affected by the influence of nearby Pompeii and Herculaneum when they began to be uncovered in the mid-18th century, and the neoclassical architectural detailing in the decoration of interiors is a result of the excitement aroused by the discovery of complete rooms filled with frescoed motifs.

Below Naples the coastal road between Sorrento, Positano, Ravello, and Amalfi winds through a landscape that many Italians think is the most beautiful of all. Here, too, villas cling to the hillside, and the views of fishing villages from the precipitous coastal road are enchanting. Flowering pots of oleander, geraniums, and exotic subtropical plants fill every tiny space. Arbors drip with bougainvillea, and long lazy lunches are eaten in their shade. Life is enjoyed outside for as long as the season allows. It makes a very colorful scene, enhanced by the exterior painting of all houses, each one different from its neighbor.

Much of the architecture of southern Italy and Sicily is driven by the need to keep out the scorching summer sun; houses have thick walls and small windows so that they stay cool even on the hottest days. In Apulia, a region in the heel of Italy, rounded pepper-pot houses called *trulli* are unique to the area. Constructed from dry-stone blocks, they have cone-shaped roofs that are hung with gray tiles. The *trulli* usually have whitewashed walls both on the exterior—to reflect the sun—and inside—to maximize the light, since the windows are very small.

One of the main businesses in this region is the production of ceramics, both for the table—in the form of plates, mugs, pitchers, and so on—and tiling for floors and walls. This is a craft industry at which the Italians have excelled since the Middle Ages. Now, as then, it is a thriving export trade, and Italian pottery and tiles decorated with traditional and contemporary images are easy to find all over the world. Rooms in Sicily are often decorated with thousands of beautifully patterned and colored tiles, which create an arresting effect when seen *en masse*, as one set of tiles competes for prominence with the next. The often-faded grandeur of Sicily's great palaces and villas harks back to the days of baroque splendor when the land was prosperous, calling to mind the vivid descriptions of an aristocratic boyhood in Giuseppe di Lampedusa's novel *Il Gattopardo* (*The Leopard*).

Perched on a cliff high above the sea, the view from the Villa Rufolo in Ravenna is among the most spectacular on this dramatic coastline. The steeply wooded hillside tumbles down to the sea. Beaches, formed in tiny inlets, are surrounded by small fishing villages, many of which are now fashionable resorts.

THE ESSENCE
OF ITALIAN STYLE

Italian rooms are often beautifully proportioned: the height of the
ceiling, the size and layout of the architectural features—the fireplace,
windows, and doors—have all been carefully calculated to create a sense
of harmony and balance. Similar care is taken when furnishing a room.
Furniture and pictures can be placed in such a way to emphasize the
balance, with matching pairs arranged symmetrically, like mirror
images. But equilibrium does not always dictate arrangement in pairs.
Sometimes harmony is suggested by placing different, but balanced,
objects in the room as if an old-fashioned scale was loaded with a number
of small objects on one side and a single massive object on the other, but each
of equal weight. Italians seem to do this as much by instinct as by design.
Perhaps it is in the blood—a cultural tradition that reaches back to the
Romans must have affected the creation of Italian taste and style.

The elegant proportions of this room are echoed in the balanced
arrangement of the furniture, placed in pairs on each side
of the long sofa. Tall windows fill the room with light,
reflected in the 18th-century Venetian chandelier.

WALLS

The walls in most Italian homes are colored white to reflect the light and to form a plain but effective backdrop to the dark wood furniture and terracotta floors that are two of the other key elements in simple Italian style. However, the Italians are also known for their love of theatrical extravagance, and in many historic interiors every possible surface is covered with pattern and color.

Walls painted with frescoes and *trompe-l'oeil* have been a vital feature of Italian decorative style since the Renaissance, when interest in the ancient Roman sites was awakened (see page 11). Generations of artists have copied the ideas found there and developed their own techniques for *trompe-l'oeil* and fresco painting of all kinds. Architectural embellishment, *faux* country and garden scenes, make-believe marble, carved stone, and moldings have been painted to give the opulence of extravagant materials without the expense.

Italian craftsmen still paint copies of fine marbles with such perfect realism that it is possible to be fooled. In some circumstances, exact reproduction of the original material is not appropriate, but they are skilled at painting with a freedom that captures the spirit of marble without precisely replicating it. This technique is often used to form a dado on the wall or an architrave around the doors and windows. Sometimes marble *trompe-l'oeil* columns are painted at intervals along the wall, appearing to support the ceiling, while the spaces in between may be filled with pastoral scenes or long vistas into the garden or countryside beyond. This makes the room seem lighter and more spacious, while introducing a sensation of *rus in urbe* to a city dwelling.

Trompe-l'oeil painting techniques are also used to create the effect of moldings and architectural importance in a room that is otherwise plain, to give the impression of richness. The device can be quite simple, with lines in varying strengths of color to indicate the profile of the molding and the direction of the light source, or it can be more intricately drawn to look like deeply carved decorative friezes. Panels are painted with baroque decorative devices, rococo swirls, or neoclassical formalism, depending on the style of the room.

Wall painting is not always meant to trick the eye. Sometimes it is intended as a joyful exuberance appealing to the Italian sense of theatricality. For instance, the walls of the long entrance hall to Bianchi-Bandinelli, a country villa outside Siena, are covered with scenes of rural revelry, painted with such vigor that the spectator feels like joining in the dancing (see pages 52–3). They are intended not as *trompe-l'oeils*, but more as a painted celebration of the pleasures of country living.

Stencil techniques are a less extravagant way of decorating and present the opportunity of introducing pattern to the walls. The effect can be particularly dramatic if the motif is repeated—as at the Palazzo Davanzati in Florence, where the walls are painted with a mixture of boldly colored lozenge designs and other regularly repeating motifs, which almost looks like wallpaper. Stenciled borders are particularly effective if they are embellished by hand.

In spite of this love of extravagant decoration, it is also possible to find perfectly simple houses with no wall decoration at all, not even rough plaster or a coat of paint. Exposed stone can be just as much a decorative statement as an intricately painted wall, but when done deliberately it can point to a rejection of the sophistication of interior decoration, and may be seen as an expression of the desire to return to the naturalism of rural roots and an uncomplicated way of life.

Rustic realism can be a stage more finished when rendered with rough white plaster or stucco. This is the most common wall treatment in Italy and can be seen everywhere, from city apartments and townhouses to country homes and oceanside dwellings. Stucco is made from a mixture of cement, sand, and lime, the finish depending on the quality of the sand. The finest sand results in the smoothest finish, but the most usual finish is a fairly rough white wall.

The simplicity of this style of wall decoration is far more in sympathy with current fashionable trends for minimalism than the highly embellished decoration of ancestral houses. Sometimes it is a considered decorative choice; sometimes it is more a question of neglecting to choose anything else. But either way it provides a setting that works well for the display of objects and pictures, and lets the

The walls of this room in an Umbrian village house were painted with a dazzling fresco in the 19th century. It depicts heavy draped curtains that have been raised to reveal an imaginary street scene. The three-dimensional effect is heightened by the solid look of the *faux* marble dado and the *trompe-l'oeil* stonework. The fresco continues around the room (see page 115).

architectural features of the room speak for themselves. One Italian device that is often used to complete the decoration, however, is to paint a "baseboard" about 10 inches high all around the room, between floor and wall, in a medium gray paint to define the border and give the room a proper finish, like framing a picture. It also has a practical purpose—it hides scuff marks that would otherwise show up against the white wall.

Less frequently seen, colorwashing is a natural progression from plain white walls, and it works particularly well in coastal and rural houses. Sometimes the color is added to the plaster as it is applied; alternatively, a diluted tinted limewash is loosely brushed over the surface afterward. Thinned paint can be used in the same way, leaving the lively effect of brushstrokes texturing the surface. Paint in Italy can be bought in powdered pigment form, ready to be mixed with whatever base is required for the purpose. A natural effect is achieved when a handful of earth is thrown into plaster as it is mixed and then applied to the wall. This results in a soft and gentle terracotta color.

A more sophisticated technique for walls is *stucco lustro*—a diluted mixture of plaster and lime applied in thin layers and then polished with beeswax, which gives a perfectly smooth finish that glows with a deep mellow luster. *Calce rosata*, which is put on with a spatula in several increasingly thin coats, then smoothed to a highly polished surface with the application of milk, looks freer, with little gray specks in the surface.

Elaborate stucco work is a special feature of walls and ceilings in historic interiors. Often the scheme for the walls continues onto the ceiling, and the whole design is conceived as a single entity. Italian *stuccatore*, the skilled practitioners of the art of plaster molding, were famed throughout Europe and used to travel widely fulfilling commissions. Their abilities varied greatly, and whereas in the great palaces this form of sculptural decoration displays a finesse that is second to none, in simpler villas and hunting lodges the design and execution is more naïve and robust. In its most opulent form, it shows entire figures formed from plaster, arranged so they appear to be supporting the ceiling or propped up languorously along the arched pediment of a door.

The walls in Italian interiors are usually painted using one technique or another, but there are also rooms hung with tapestries, finely woven silks, or wallpapers. The finest tapestries were imported into Italy from Flanders and France. By the 16th century, several Flemish weavers had been paid to set up their looms in Italy, and tapestries were produced in Ferra, Florence, and Mantua. In 1627 the Barberini factory was founded in Rome to weave tapestries for the Papal and Barberini palaces, and in 1731 the Turin factory began producing hangings for the House of Savoy. In all these cases, biblical or mythological subjects were popular, as were reminders of illustrious historical events.

As an alternative, many grand palaces with 18th-century decoration (such as the Palazzo Pallavicini Rospigliosi in Rome) have walls in their principal rooms hung with brilliantly colored silks. Such materials create a lustrous, yet almost plain expanse of color on the walls, the flat effect broken only by the weave and light-reflecting qualities of the material.

Wallpaper is generally a less luxurious finish, which is found most often in houses that were built or redecorated in the 19th century. Wallpapers were imported from France at the end of the 18th century and introduced a delicate elegance to the interiors where they were hung. Later papers were robustly patterned with scrolls or damask designs, often intended to emulate the rich Venetian silks that were hung on the walls of the most luxurious *palazzi*. *Faux* leather wallpaper, printed to look like expensive Spanish leather, fulfills the same purpose. The Italian passion for *trompe-l'oeil* meant that the incredibly effective wallpapers made by the Zuber factory in 19th-century France found a popular market in Italy, and it is not unusual to find walls hung with what appears at first sight to be sumptuous draperies complete with deeply fringed passementeries and tassels, which in fact turn out to be highly extravagant wallpaper.

The sheer magnificence and scale of their decorative ideas means that Italians are not great do-it-yourself enthusiasts, and in every town and city there are many skilled craftsmen trained in traditional skills who can apply whatever finish is required to the walls, from plain stucco to subtle marbling, graining, and other *trompe-l'oeil* techniques, and who are also experienced at restoration.

When restoring this Tuscan farmhouse, the owners were at great pains to retain the atmosphere created by the generations who had lived and worked here before. The rough plaster walls are finished with a surface of chalk mixed with sand and earth taken from the ground outside the house.

Wall treatments in Italy range from simple white plaster and colorwashes to the more polished surfaces of *stucco lustro* and *marmorino*, painted *trompe-l'oeil*, and fresco. Most of them are beautifully executed by artists and decorators who are often using techniques that have been handed down through the generations. Some of the effects, such as a simple *trompe-l'oeil* panel, are quick and cheap to achieve, and give depth and interest to a wall, but others demand a greater skill and commitment. Wallpapers and tapestries add visual diversity and texture to a room, while molded plasterwork introduces a particularly decorative rhythm to the surface of the wall.

CEILINGS

Decorating the ceiling is a forgotten art in modern interiors. Nowadays most people paint the ceiling white and leave it at that, but in Italy the ceiling often forms part of the overall design scheme. It stems from the influence of the great Italian artists commissioned to decorate the palaces of their patrons with magnificent frescoes, but the idea reaches out to much less sophisticated rural villas and hunting lodges, where the ceilings may be covered with painted clouds, flower-bedecked trellises, or astonishing *trompe-l'oeil* moldings that form an architectural framework. Sometimes playful cherubs and gaily costumed people enliven the scene. It is a strange sensation, but very convivial, to wake up in a room filled with jolly characters cavorting on the ceiling.

The ceilings of renaissance palaces often have visible beams: massive structures spanning the width of the room and gloriously decorated with painted patterns or stenciled motifs, with liberal amounts of gold leaf added for good measure. Their constructional purpose is often masked by cross beams formed to create deeply coffered ceilings with carved embellishments, making a checkerboard pattern on the ceiling.

In simpler rural interiors, the beams are natural wood, and their function of supporting the floor above is clearly visible. A lighter effect is achieved when the beams are painted with a diluted whitewash, but it is more traditional to see natural terracotta and dark wood. The most expensive beams are made from hefty chestnut trees, so in cases when pine is used in restorations for reasons of economy, the beams look far more authentic when they are stained a deep rich shade of brown.

This dining room ceiling (opposite) has been stenciled with a delicate palmette design—a motif that has its origins in ancient Greece, was adopted by the Romans, and is replicated in various forms of architecture and decoration all over Italy. Classical references also appear in this frieze (above right), which extends upward to a frescoed, vaulted ceiling.

The ceiling beams are often visible in Italian homes. Sometimes the massive chestnut supports have been left plain (right), while at other times they have been decorated (background).

FLOORS

Beautiful floors are an integral part of Italian interior style. Terracotta is universally used, while glazed ceramic floors are frequently seen in kitchens and bathrooms, particularly in southern Italy.

Marble floors are often laid in wonderfully intricate patterns that make a dazzling statement. The wide variety of marble colors—black and dark green, russet red, raw sienna, terracotta, ocher, saffron, creamy pink, and the palest of yellows, grays, buffs, and milky whites with all the various hues in between, veined with the strange natural gradations of color—give this extraordinary material its character. To make one of these impressive floors, differently colored marbles, chosen to contrast with each other, are cut into various shapes and fitted together with as little grout as possible to make a perfectly smooth surface. The design may follow the style of decoration on the walls or ceiling. It can be a repeating geometric pattern, or a more fluid series of interlinking curls and flourishes that owes much to baroque influence.

Italy is home to a great marble industry and sends this precious material all over the world, wherever there is a demand for luxury. The purest, whitest marble comes from the quarries at Carrara, above Pisa, where sculptors from Michelangelo to Henry Moore have found unblemished chunks from which to carve. In new apartments, offices, stores, and houses, a pale travertine marble floor is commonplace, chosen not only for its beauty but also for its practicality. Contemporary architects like marble for its elegant simplicity and are just as likely to use it on walls as floors.

Marble is also used in terrazzo. This kind of flooring is made from marble chips mixed with bits of crushed stone and stucco. It is traditionally laid in thin layers and then crushed down and laboriously polished to a shiny surface. Nowadays it can also be laid in tile form. Sometimes, in very old interiors, chips of semiprecious minerals, such as lapis lazuli and malachite, are sprinkled among the marble pieces. Terrazzo can be laid simply, with the same color and texture from one side of the room to the other, or it can be laid in patterns of swirling shapes. Some families have their crest defined in different shades of terrazzo, but normally it gives a less immediately spectacular effect than marble. Like marble it looks immensely heavy and rigid, but it is in fact a rather flexible surface and bends with the movement of the building over time.

Ceramic tiles also make a very heavy and durable floor. Brightly glazed and patterned tiles are an essential component of Italian interiors and are found all over the country, particularly south of Rome, in Naples, and in Sicily. The colors are dazzling—very clear pigments under a high-gloss glaze made from molten glass, which enhances the color as if it is continually wet. The numerous patterns are inspired by a variety of sources, including oriental design, nature, ancient Roman motifs, traditional designs, geometric arrangements, and abstract shapes. Tiles are used on floors and walls all over the house. Handmade tiles are particularly attractive, especially when they are glazed white. The top surface of such a tile has a slightly uneven surface, which results in a barely noticeable mottled effect that is enhanced when the glaze melts to varying thicknesses in the firing.

Mosaic—a design or decoration made from small pieces of colored glass, stone, or tile arranged in a bed of cement or *cocciopesto*—was developed by the Egyptians. The Romans used it extensively on their floors and walls, but as decoration it reached its zenith during the late 16th century, with the massive works for St. Peter's Basilica in Rome. Today, mosaic is found mainly in Italian bathrooms and swimming pools, where its luminous quality is enhanced by reflections in the water.

If one color could be said to capture the feel of Italy, it is terracotta. Terracotta tiles are made from natural clay that is baked hard in the kiln, hence the name, which means "baked earth." Making tiles is a craft that traces its origins back to the Etruscans. Tiles vary in color according to the place the earth comes from, the length of the firing process, and the intensity of the heat. A very hot kiln produces a lighter golden color than a cooler one, where the result is a rich reddish-brown. Age also has an effect—old roof tiles are bleached by the sun and, with time, acquire the color of crusty bread. Manufactured tiles are more uniform in color, size, and texture, which is why people who are restoring rural buildings go to so much trouble to find old tiles.

Because terracotta tiles have always been so universally available and practical for floors, myriad styles and patterns have evolved. This makes it possible to lay both simple patterns and designs of some complexity. Often a plain border is laid around the room, two tiles thick, and then a more interesting pattern, perhaps a herringbone or basketweave, is laid in the middle. Such floors are kept polished to a perfect luster and will last for centuries, their deep organic color providing a warm and comforting base for the decoration of the rest of the room.

Wooden floors are less often seen in Italy, though when they are laid they are highly prized and beautifully maintained. They can be long, wide chestnut planks, laid simply side by side and lovingly polished over the years to a deep umber brown, or they can be lighter parquet, laid in chevron patterns, basketweaves, and squares made from ever-diminishing lengths of wood. These floors have a special smell and creak gently as the passage of feet causes the wooden joints to move. They call for an abundance of oriental rugs, which Italians have loved since the Venetians and the Genoese began importing them from Persia in medieval times. Rush matting makes a practical alternative, and is often found in country houses. Carpet is usually noticeable for its absence. A carpet may be found in the bedroom of a new apartment, but most Italians prefer the sense of spaciousness created by a beautiful floor and a few rugs.

THIS PAGE AND BACKGROUND Patterned floors are made from a variety of materials including terrazzo (background), glazed and unglazed tiles (above right), and colored marble (right).

OVERLEAF LEFT Terracotta tiles, made from clay baked in an oven, are the most popular form of flooring in Italy. These old handmade tiles have been laid in a herringbone pattern, which is emphasized by the slight differences in color between each tile and its neighbor.

OVERLEAF RIGHT Colored marble tiles have been cut into geometric shapes and laid to create a *trompe-l'oeil* pattern on the floor of the Ridotto in Venice.

FABRICS

Fine Italian cloth is famous all over the world. Lustrous silks, rich velvets, handwoven brocades, both thick and delicate lacework, and crisp linens add depth and color to interiors throughout the country.

Damask is perhaps the most influential of all the designs inherited from the past and in continuous demand today. The effect of tone on tone, of lighter and darker shades of the same color created by the weave, makes for a rich and vibrant cloth that catches the light in its folds and creates the illusion of movement. It can be startlingly opulent, especially when the silk is woven in claret red, deep forest green, or dazzling Naples yellow. In the past, the most lavish of damask silks were widely used to cover walls as part of the decoration in important rooms (see page 34). The seating, which was positioned against the walls, was often upholstered in the same silk to make a completely unified scheme.

Silks of this quality and richness have always been a luxury, and different means have been tried to simulate the effect without the cost. Artificial fibers are used, cottons are woven instead of silk, and the damask motif is often printed on fabric instead of being woven into it. One of the most successful simulations was made in the 1920s by Mario Fortuny in Venice, who developed a secret technique for handprinting the lustrous effect of damask. His work, which is still available in Venice, London, and New York, is now prized as a unique and special material in its own right.

The silk weavers of northern Italy have been perfecting their art for centuries, reproducing patterns from historical archives and creating completely contemporary designs. Both are appreciated, for just as there are many owners of historic houses anxious to keep as closely as possible to the most appropriate designs for their rooms, so there are large numbers of people living in cities, whose enthusiasm is for all things modern. Italian designers are imaginative exponents of contemporary design, and this can be seen as much in their textiles as in their furniture. Exciting weaves are created with interesting mixtures of textures, combined with highly experimental fibers. The more exotic of these designs are displayed as wall hangings, while simpler designs are used for upholstery.

Thick velvets in jewel-bright colors, complex woven tapestries, and traditional bargello designs are frequently used to upholster couches, chairs, and pillows because they are strong and hard-wearing, but also have a luxurious feel. Originally the finest velvets were made from silk, with its unique luster and depth of color. Today, cotton is more frequently used, and artificial fibers have also been developed to simulate the richness of silk velvet.

Prints and textured weaves are also used for upholstery, but the use of fabrics in extravagant drapery treatments is less common in Italy than in other parts of Europe and the United States. Windows invariably have shutters to keep out the strong sunshine in the summer, and these can be firmly closed for added warmth in winter, reducing the practical need for curtains. It is part of the look of Italian style that interest focuses on the walls, the floors, the ceiling, and the furniture, with the windows being regarded as part of the structure of the room, rather than a feature needing decorative treatment. Occasionally light gauze or linen curtains break this rule, or canvas shades are drawn to shield the sun, but there is none of the frilly frippery—the swags and tails, gathers, pintucks, pleated headings, and other curtain treatments—that is the stock in trade of many decorators outside Italy.

Lace, which provides the exception to this rule, is seen in windows in the very north of Italy, where the influence is more Austrian or Swiss, in alpine regions and by the lakes. It is also highly prized for bed hangings and table linen. Lace is a traditional specialty of Lombardy, where some of the earliest handmade examples have been recorded, and beautiful antique and contemporary lace are frequently found in this region as bedspreads or made into covers for pillows. When a lace cover is thrown over a white cotton fabric, the effect is of a crunchy texture like icing sugar on a cake, but another dimension is created when the fabric beneath is a different color and the design woven into the lace becomes more prominent. The same contrast is apparent with a perfectly laundered lace tablecloth on a polished dark wood table.

Linen is another fabric that is seen in bedrooms and dining rooms throughout Italy, and it is common practice for Italians to have the very best linen they can afford. Fresh napkins, heavy tablecloths, and crisp sheets are washed and ironed with loving care, so that they last for years. White is universally the favorite color for such items, its simple purity a restful contrast to brightly colored surroundings.

Italian fabrics are renowned throughout the world for their rich colors, sensuous textures, and historic designs. Beautiful silk damasks have been woven in Italy for centuries, and since the 1920s their designs have been famously replicated in cotton using Mario Fortuny's secret technique. Voluptuous silk velvets take on an even richer appearance when appliquéd with braid, and passementerie tassels, twisted cords, and rosettes finish silk upholstery with a typical flourish.

FURNITURE

Italians have a tendency to keep things in the family, so a house that has been lived in for generations may contain an eclectic mixture of furniture. The same happens with families who may not be living in their ancestral home but have inherited furniture from their parents, grandparents, uncles, or aunts.

Of course, it is rare anywhere to see rooms entirely furnished with antiques from one period, unless they are museums; most people have a fairly varied assortment in their homes. In Italy the style also depends on the area, because furniture design differs according to region almost as much as to period.

In the north, particularly in the alpine regions, the Austrian influence helped to define a style of painted wooden furniture known as *arte povera*. Simple wooden pieces are freely painted with bright colors and then decorated with the vigorous floral motifs of folk art, a technique that livens up the piece and makes it appropriate for simple rustic interiors.

A little farther south, in the Lombardy region, there is a lot of wrought iron, which may have been introduced to the region in the 16th century by the Spanish. Wrought iron is a surprisingly versatile material and can be used equally effectively to create swirling balustrades on a grand staircase or a delicate pair of candle sconces. It is also frequently found as the legs to wooden- or marble-topped tables.

Probably the most widespread use of wrought iron in Italy is in beds. The traditional *letto matrimoniale* (double bed) is high off the ground, with a headboard and base made from curving shapes of iron. Sometimes a decorative roundel is incorporated into the center and painted with a pastoral scene, a floral decoration, or even the coat of arms of the owner. Wrought iron's practical and robust qualities, as well as its ability to be highly decorative, make it an ideal material for outdoor furniture, such as chairs, benches, and tables. It is not, however, especially comfortable, so pillows upholstered in strong cotton or canvas are usually added to make the long hours spent eating and relaxing outside more pleasurable.

The Italians are very talented at display and have an ability to arrange decorative objects in a way that commands attention. This is sometimes done by grouping many similar pieces—such as interesting glass or silver—in close proximity, and sometimes by mixing an assorted group of objects, so that each item complements the others. Occasionally this is achieved so skillfully that the result is like a three-dimensional still life.

The thoughtful hanging of pictures is a vital part of the overall harmony of the room. Whether they are the priceless work of an Italian Master, handed down through the generations, or inexpensive prints and engravings bought at a local antiques store or market, they are always arranged with careful attention to symmetry and balance: family portraits may be hung in pairs; an important oil painting will be placed centrally on a wall with furniture arranged to balance it; and a series of prints will be displayed together for decorative impact.

Lighting in Italy is an intriguing subject, for it would appear that many Italians spend much of their time indoors in relative gloom. Not only are the shutters kept closed during the heat of the day, but also few lights are turned on in the evening (this might have something to do with the extortionate cost of electricity). When they are being used, Italian lamps can look very effective. Some of the best have functioned previously as church candlesticks and have been converted to take electricity. They are attractively carved and often gilded. When placed against the wall, they may be topped by half-shades that cover only the front of the bulb. Often the shades are finished with a print pasted on the surface for decoration.

Distinct styles of furniture are associated with many of Italy's major cities. In Florence, heavy, carved wooden furniture is characteristic, while 18th-century Naples is renowned for the opulence of its gilded chairs and console tables. Much Venetian furniture was carved and lavishly gilded; sets of chairs and benches were upholstered with expensive silks; and console tables, with their characteristic slightly splayed legs, were arranged beneath matching ornate and equally gilded mirrors.

Venetian lacquered furniture is more instantly recognizable and was one of the most desirable items to be brought back from a visit to Venice in the 18th century. It was a very costly, skilled, and time-consuming technique, and its very expense meant that it was rapidly copied using less extravagant materials and the rather clever deception of découpage. Instead of using an artist's skills in painted decoration and the painstaking build-up of lacquer, the maker glued little motifs, which he cut out from purpose-made printed paper, onto the piece of furniture and then covered them with so many layers of varnish that the edge of the paper disappeared and the piece looked like expensive lacquerware. These pretty pieces are now very desirable, and the technique is still used today.

The dark wood of Tuscan furniture is considerably more sturdy in appearance than these delicate painted Venetian pieces, and it fits appropriately into rural houses. Antique pieces are especially sought, particularly the deep, highly-carved chests used for storing clothes and blankets in the summer months. Armoires and cupboards have a bulk that looks right with the terracotta floors, the white walls, and the wooden beams of these rustic houses. Simple straight-backed chairs with rush seats are characteristic of this area; more important chairs follow a similar high-backed style, but have upholstered seats and backs. Savonarola and Dante chairs are especially prized if they are antique. Often there is a daybed in the *salone*, made from wrought iron and with a mattress prettily covered in a traditional checked or striped material. In country houses the furniture is fairly sparsely arranged, consisting of just the pieces that are necessary for living, without too much clutter, pillows, and decorative ornaments, making for a feeling of spaciousness that characterizes Italian interiors.

RIGHT Over time the painting on this cupboard door has worn away, revealing the grain of the wood beneath. All the elements of the painted design—the curling fronds of acanthus leaves, the lozenge, the pair of birds holding trails of beads in their beaks, and the ribbon knotted in a loose bow—were used by the ancient Romans in wall decoration and have been widely reinterpreted on painted furniture and frescoes.

OVERLEAF LEFT A dynastic marriage in the 1780s between two prominent Sienese families provided the occasion to decorate this room with wallpaper imported from Paris. It is a very rare example of an early column and arch design. The painted chair and table copy the motif in a manner that is characteristic of much 18th-century Venetian furniture.

OVERLEAF RIGHT Two marble sculptures, which were originally garden ornaments from the Veneto region, absorb the pink glow of the afternoon sun. The 18th-century mirror was made in Murano, and the console table, though new, is made in typical Venetian form with gilded legs and a *faux* marble top.

THIS PAGE A heavily studded dark wooden door presents a forbidding appearance, but it is linked in style to the robustly carved *cassone*, or chest, which is now used for storing linen.

OPPOSITE An early 18th-century lacquer chair is placed on each side of a *cassone* that is ornately decorated with panels of carved, painted, and gilded gesso. Above the chest hangs a 16th-century Flemish tapestry depicting the story of Pomona (the Italian goddess of gardens and fruit trees) and Vertumnus (the god of the changing year and the giver of fruits). Vertumnus loved Pomona, and so pursued her in various shapes until he won her in the guise of a beautiful youth.

BENVENUTO

Entrance Halls and Stairways

THE ENTRANCE TO A HOUSE is conventionally indicated by some sort of architectural flourish—a porch, an important architrave or pediment, a short flight of steps, a small garden, or a path—to give it emphasis and to indicate that this is the point of arrival. However imposing, these architectural features and the arrangement of doors and windows normally conspire to give an agreeable, welcoming aspect. But in Italy this is often not the case, especially in the center of old towns where historic houses, great and small, open directly onto the street. The windows of these buildings are high and often latticed with iron bars, and the huge wooden doors are constructed from thick wide planks that are joined horizontally and studded with iron nails. Indeed, it is quite possible to walk straight past the austere walls of an important medieval or renaissance *palazzo* without even realizing it.

Once inside the forbidding exterior, however, the outlook softens. Often the doors open onto a courtyard, which may be beautifully planted and graced by statues, stone benches, a fountain, or even a well. Sometimes there will be an exterior staircase that sweeps visitors upward to the main reception rooms, which are usually located on the *piano nobile* (second floor).

By the end of the 16th century, it had become customary for the important urban families to build villas as country retreats. Here, the entrance was altogether more welcoming. In the famous Villa Giulia, built in 1550 by Giacomo Barozzi da Vignola for Pope Julius III in what was then the countryside outside Rome, a curved colonnade opens like two arms, linking the garden to the house and inspiring a sense of relaxation and welcome. This idea was also used by Andrea Palladio in the Villa Badoer in the Veneto, although it is more usual for his villas to have a wide flight of steps leading from the garden to a classical *portico* of columns and pediment, or perhaps to an open *loggia* with tall rounded arches, such as those at the Villa Saraceno.

Visitors entering on the ground floor may be surprised by the simplicity of the internal staircase. This is particularly true of houses such as Villa Cetinale, where the main stairs are on the outside of the building. The stairs at Villa Bianchi-Bandinelli, on the other hand, are wide and imposing—perhaps because there is no external staircase with which to compete for attention. The steps in old and important buildings are usually made from stone or marble, while others are in wood, tile or, in some contemporary conversions, metal. The type of handrail provided is also a question of style, and can vary between a loosely tied rope and an iron or wooden rail. In very grand establishments, the rail is sometimes a hollow niche that has been carved from the wall itself.

PREVIOUS PAGES The entrance hall of Villa Bianchi-Bandinelli at Geggiano, near Siena, was painted with scenes of rural revelry by the artist Ignazio Moder at the end of the 18th century. The activities of the changing seasons—harvesting, winemaking, and hunting—and their associated festivals are depicted in a continuous theme around the walls, and portraits of the family mingle with those of local celebrities. Entering this hall you become part of the fresco, with the sky above you, the landscape beyond, and all the figures welcoming you to join their celebrations.

At the other end of the vaulted corridor, the door into the garden is propped open by a lump of pumice stone. Beside it, a traditionally painted pottery jar contains a clutch of walking sticks, ready for a stroll around the garden, while in the corner, a nursing chair can be recognized by its generously open arms.

OPPOSITE The entrance to this *palazzo* is simply but beautifully furnished with four carved walnut chairs and two 17th-century Flemish tapestries. Sun floods in through the circular glass in the leaded windowpanes, producing a gently diffused light during the day. At night the tall wrought-iron and bronze lamps, with their typically Italian vellum half-shades, cast pools of light around the room. The highly polished wooden floor, laid in a chevron pattern, creaks gently as you walk across it.

OPPOSITE The noble scale of the *sala* (hall) in Villa Saraceno in the Veneto was designed by Palladio using classical measurements of proportion.

The arresting frieze underneath the decorated ceiling beams contrasts with the plain ivory walls below. It depicts, in a series of cartouches, theatrical scenes being played out in front of classical façades. The changing scales of the fresco create the illusion of pierced windows through which the activity can be seen.

The floor was originally laid in 1612 and has recently been restored. It is made using a Venetian technique known as *battuto*, where building materials are crushed with lime, ground smooth, and oiled. The effect is like a robust and rustic form of terrazzo.

OVERLEAF The ground floor hall in Villa Cetinale has a high vaulted ceiling and traditionally painted white walls, which reflect the light streaming in from the garden and further enhance the feeling of space (right). A narrow stone staircase leads up from the hall to the *piano nobile*, where the main reception rooms are situated. The walls of the hall are hung with pictures, including a page from an illuminated manuscript, a portrait, and a mirror, while up the stairs a group of contemporary watercolors show some of the dozens of mushroom varieties to be found around Siena.

Hanging on the other side of the same hall (left) is an 18th-century painting of an idealized landscape, showing energetic huntsmen and dogs in active pursuit of their quarry. In the background, undulating hills rise to mountains in the far distance, in a way that is reminiscent of much Italian scenery. The chest below it displays a diverse collection of objects, including a bust, an animal skull, and a porcupine quill.

It is rare to find carpet on the stairs in Italy—most are left bare and kept beautifully polished. If the staircase is particularly precipitous, a hard-wearing runner is sometimes laid and kept in place by metal stair rods.

Arriving at a *palazzo* in Venice is a unique experience. A gondola transports visitors across the water to a flight of steps outside the building, onto which they can alight whatever the state of the tide. Once inside the entrance, the scene is rather dark and gloomy. It was here that the merchant stored the goods that his ships had carried home to Venice, and the rooms on either side have a practical purpose unsuited for entertainment. So visitors are swiftly transported upstairs and welcomed in a room known in the city as the *portico*, a long wide hall that stretches from one end of the *palazzo* to the other.

Traditionally, many Tuscan farmhouses had their living quarters on the second floor, while the cattle and other animals were housed below. Entrance to the upstairs was again via steps that ran up the outside of the building. A similar arrangement occurs in the mountain farmhouses of northern Italy. When the animals were brought down from their summer pastures to winter, they were kept in the shelter of the farmhouse, protected from the snow and icy temperatures, and fed on hay, which was also stored there. Today many of the original stables have been converted into rooms for the skiers who flock to the region during the season. The exterior stairways now lead up to typical Tyrolean wood fretwork balconies, which are picturesque places on which to welcome friends, sit in the winter sun, and drink a glass of hot wine after a strenuous day on the *piste*.

Wherever you are in Italy, there is generally little furniture in the hall, reflecting the fact that it is a place used to receive guests rather than somewhere to linger and chat. Chairs and benches may be arranged around the walls, but they are often selected on looks rather than comfort—soft armchairs are much more likely to be found in the living room. As elsewhere in Italian houses, the tendency is for furniture to be grouped in pairs, or arrangements that balance on each side of the room, and pictures are hung in the same way to create a sense of harmony.

For all this variety of architectural style and grandeur, what is really most noticeable when you visit an Italian home is the strength of the welcome that you receive and the ease with which strangers are absorbed into the bosom of the family. It is a genuine expression of hospitality, springing from a characteristic generosity of spirit and warmth of personality, which is such a delightful characteristic of the Italian people.

OPPOSITE Broad horizontal stripes in yellow and rust give this small hall a touch of wit and drama. The colors are picked up again, more conventionally, in the door moldings. An old painted Tyrolean chest provides useful storage space. It is topped by a contemporary pitcher from Deruta, which is decorated in traditional style.

THIS PAGE An ancient wooden door, made in the age-old way from wide planks studded with iron nails, has been given a new lease on life by a vibrant coat of paint. The same color has also been applied, rather charmingly, to the chair inside the door. The walls and floor have been kept in the state in which they were found, by someone who appreciates their naturalness—much character can be lost by overworked restoration.

OVERLEAF LEFT The basic elements of this second floor landing are simple—a natural terracotta floor and plain iron railings to shield the stone staircase. An unexpected air of sophistication is provided by the set of *verre églomisé* plates hung on the walls. This technique involves gold leaf being applied to the back of a glass plate, so that it gives a brilliantly sparkling surface. The effect is enhanced by the walls being painted pale yellow, a color that has a natural welcoming feel.

OVERLEAF RIGHT A lavish treatment of raised stucco moldings, marble door frames, lively colors, and intricate geometric floor tiles compete for attention in this hall. This is the *portico* of a house built for pleasure—it was originally a Venetian gaming house, so during its history it undoubtedly has been the scene of many a riotous evening. Nowadays it is the headquarters of the Alliance française, whose academic and cultural gatherings are of a more sober nature.

The furniture arranged around the walls is characteristically Venetian, with its painted wooden frames and cane seats.

OPPOSITE A wide stone stairway in a country villa leads from the hall on the ground floor to the main reception rooms above. The loosely tied rope stands out against the gently distressed wall, which is painted in olive leaf green. On the bottom pillar, a *trompe-l'oeil* painting in grisaille gives the effect of three-dimensional molding on a pilaster, while a traditional painted baseboard runs up the stairs.

THIS PAGE A simpler form of support, but more secure, is offered by this iron rod, firmly gripped by the brass hand that guides the way to the upstairs of this restored farmhouse near Todi.

CONVERSAZIONE

Salons and
Living Rooms

PREVIOUS PAGES LEFT The light-filled *salone* in this Venetian *palazzo* represents the essence of understated elegance with its restrained color palette and careful arrangement of furniture. The walls glow with a luminosity achieved by the *marmorino* technique, which produces a creamy sheen with a luster matched only by the dazzle of the terrazzo floor. Delicate, clear glass drops hanging from the arms of the chandelier, and the candelabra in the corner of the room adds to the lively diffusion of sunlight.

PREVIOUS PAGES RIGHT Two distinct motifs from classical antiquity—the egg and dart frieze and the palmette design—used here as a molding, illustrate the long history attached to the decorative ornamentation embellishing Italian houses. Such motifs are part of a design vocabulary that emerges in different guises with succeeding generations, and which has influenced interiors far beyond the borders of Italy.

OPPOSITE A magnificent 19th-century daybed, covered in sumptuous raspberry and gold woven silk, dominates this room and invites a lazy siesta. Just to its side, a chair has been pulled up to hold a book and a glass of wine.

A 16th-century Flemish tapestry fills the wall and is topped by a shade that can be let down to shield it from the strong light. Beneath it is a carved Italian wooden chest and a French 18th-century armchair.

THE LIVING ROOM, *salone,* or *salotto,* has to be one of the most flexible rooms in the house: a formal but comfortable place in which to entertain friends, and also somewhere to sit, listen to music, or read a book.

Grand country villas and city *palazzi* often have a variety of rooms in which to receive guests and to relax. Walls and ceilings in the finest rooms are covered with remarkable decorations, and the rooms themselves are furnished with superb antiques, paintings, and objects. These rooms have evolved through the ages along with their contents. In the 18th century, chairs and upholstered benches would have been arranged around the walls to leave a wide open space in the center of the room for people to gather, converse, and dance. During the 19th century, Empire-style chairs with stiffly upholstered backs and seats were arranged in a group around a table, indicating an altogether more prim and polite style of communication between the guests. By passing these influences and artifacts down through the generations, some *palazzi* have become living museums that serve to illuminate the past.

A sense of spaciousness is common to almost all *saloni,* whatever their size and relative grandeur. This is due in part to the fact that the main rooms in an Italian house usually have high ceilings, even in relatively simple farmhouses.

In historic palaces, the imposing size and the painted decoration create reception rooms that have a unique dynamism and importance. Those artists who played tricks with light and space with skillful *trompe-l'oeil* painting made illusions of infinitely receding distance, which seem to open out the walls far beyond their actual perimeter. Rooms without these dramatic scenic paintings achieve effects of space through a completely contrary style of interior decoration—the simplest form of wall finish is plain creamy white stucco, and this technique used in a room with lofty ceilings and not too much furniture creates a similar sense of space.

The fireplace is often the focal point of a reception room—it is frequently built on a massive scale that simply demands attention. In a farmhouse, rough beams often form a heavy lintel or a hefty mantelpiece on which to display objects. In more exalted surroundings, the lintel and mantelpiece are likely to be made from carved stone, while the chimney breast may be painted with an armorial device proclaiming the family of the owner.

The treatment of the floors is another way in which to achieve a sense of space in reception rooms. Wide expanses of polished terrazzo, marble, or terracotta tiles provide an unadorned simplicity, and while it is usual to see an oriental rug or a *kilim* spread on the floor, the small area that they cover has the effect of amplifying the

OPPOSITE This house on the outskirts of Florence has been furnished to provide a comfortable place to sit and converse. Its cream marble floor is broken by square tiles in terracotta and black. The area above the molding is painted in cantaloupe, a warm color that is picked up in the cushions and the lampshades to create a welcoming and intimate feel.

OVERLEAF The stone fireplace is the focus in the *salone* of this restored farmhouse in Umbria, flanked by the bookcases and armchairs (left). Old Turkish muskets are propped against the hearth, below a painting of a southern Italian girl who is proudly holding bunches of luscious grapes. A bright pink cloth covers the table, adding a brilliant splash of color to the otherwise plain décor. Portraits of two Neapolitan ancestors hang as a pair on the other side of the room, above the antique table and chairs (right). The whole room provides a satisfying glimpse of the instinct for symmetry that infuses Italian taste.

space. A large rug is a very unusual sight, and a wall-to-wall carpet almost unheard of; the cozy feel engendered by such a carpet is not at all a feature of Italian interiors.

Furniture in the *salone* should be comfortable, but Italians also require it to be stylish. Couches often have coverings made from expensive materials in impractical colors, and old chairs get a new lease on life with white slipcovers. Daybeds are a feature of many Italian reception rooms, as some people still take a siesta during the afternoon. Other pieces of furniture that you can expect to find include built-in or freestanding bookcases (unless the house has a separate library), tables, and coffee tables.

The arrangement of furniture in the reception room is designed to facilitate easy conversation, with groups of chairs facing each other or on each side of a large sofa. Often long, low sofas are arranged to form an L or a U shape, so that chatter can flow easily back and forth, or two sofas may be arranged on each side of the fireplace, achieving a degree of comfort and informality that is part of life today.

Lighting is very important in a living room because it has to perform so many functions. Although the finest rooms are often hung with spectacular chandeliers, it is more usual to find small lamps that throw pools of light into the corners, creating a more intimate feel. Standing lamps, made from wrought iron and brass or turned wood, raise the level of the light source.

How the pictures are hung in a reception room is an important part of the creation of its style. Many Italian families own religious paintings, some of which are outstanding, and these are given prominence by their sheer size, the flamboyance of their frames, and by hanging them in the center of the wall, perhaps over a couch or an important piece of furniture. Less significant paintings or sets of prints are hung in groups where their impact is enhanced by a balanced arrangement on the wall. Even relatively inexpensive sets of prints are given this treatment, and it provides an excellent object lesson on how a good visual sense of arrangement can enhance the simplest pictures.

Italians are inveterate collectors and like to display the results of their enthusiasms in ordered arrangements around the room: on side tables, if they are objects; on the walls if they are paintings, fans, or porcelain plates; in bookshelves if they are valuable volumes of rare books. Antique silver pieces are grouped together, and beautifully decorated majolica pots, pitchers, and magnificent plates are given prominence. Antiquities from ancient Greece and Rome may form part of the display, juxtaposed with fossils and minerals of even more ancient descent.

THIS PAGE AND OPPOSITE This room is filled with the treasures of a dedicated collector (right). The wealth of exquisite objects is arranged to intrigue the intellect and delight the eye, while carefully avoiding the impression of clutter. On the stone fireplace is a collection of carvings: a pair of Greek pigeons dating from the 4th century B.C., and a Roman wild boar, rabbit, and leaping dog. Below them, a pair of fearsome 16th-century Neapolitan bull mastiffs stands guard over the hearth. Paintings with a religious theme are seen frequently in Italy, and here the figure of San Giovanni by Christofano Allori is a commanding presence. In the corner of the room (below), a marble-topped table with laurel leaves carved around its edge holds an arrangement of antiquities thrown into stark contrast by the black basalt bust.

THIS PAGE AND OPPOSITE A passion for stunning color declares the confidence of the owner who has restored the *salone* in this Umbrian village house. The cobalt blue walls drop down to a dado that is exuberantly painted with swags of shocking pink fabric, deeper tones of which are seen in the raspberry silk on the sofa. A set of *commedia dell'arte* prints, with their pink mounts and white frames, make a strong visual impact. Lapis-lazuli blue pillows echo the restored stencil decoration on the beams, and a glimpse of viridian can be seen on the balcony doors. This whole cacophony of color is tempered by the undemanding familiarity of terracotta floors and whitewash on the ceiling.

OVERLEAF LEFT Placed on the wall above a long sofa is a group of antiquities, overlorded by a carved head of Medusa from ancient Rome. Underneath it, the carved marble panel is also Roman, as is the water pitcher on the right-hand bracket. The more contrived shape of the other pitcher is 16th-century Tuscan. The couch is covered in antique Umbrian cloth that is woven with hunting scenes and laid on an ivory twill. It is completed by three velvet pillows.

OVERLEAF RIGHT A collection of 18th-century sepia prints after paintings by Claude Lorrain has been uniformly framed and hung over the couch in a type of arrangement that is frequently seen in Italian houses. Pictures grouped in this way have a stronger decorative impact than if they are spaced out around the walls.

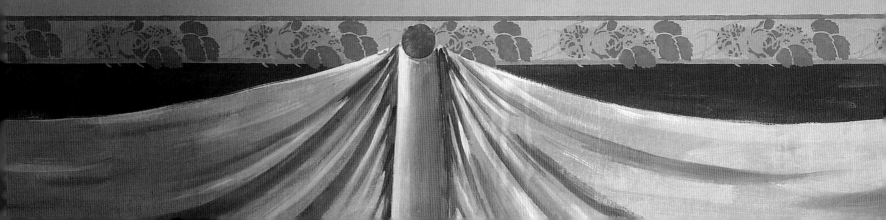

THIS PAGE AND OPPOSITE A sense of harmony is created by the mellow colors in this room (left) where the earthy walls and floors are complemented by the muted tones of the antique *kilim*. A venerable leather-covered armchair sits in the corner by the fire, which in winter is filled with huge sweet-smelling logs.

Through the open door (right), the *loggia* overlooks the courtyard outside, and old stone steps lead directly downward. In the past the farmer lived on this floor, with his animals living directly beneath him.

OVERLEAF LEFT Ocher-washed walls bring the sunshine to this converted farm building in Umbria. The traditional wide brick arch spans the room in a method of construction that is common in this part of rural Italy. On the floor, the terracotta tiles are new but traditionally handmade. The built-in seating, the blue painted baseboard and the yellow-washed walls give a contemporary twist to the restoration.

OVERLEAF RIGHT The old kitchen in this villa in the countryside near Siena has been changed into a room where all the family can sit while the cooking goes on elsewhere. During the winter, a big open fire gives visitors a traditional welcome, while in the summer a display of decorative objects brings the hearth to life. The chimney is held up on one side by a giant screw from a wine press, a reminder of the superb Chianti produced by the vineyards surrounding the villa.

DIVERTIMENTO

*Kitchens and
Dining Rooms*

CONTEMPORARY LIVING leans increasingly toward informality. Today, most lunches and dinners take the form of spontaneous gatherings of friends and family, rather than elegant formal meals that have been meticulously organized weeks in advance.

Despite this informality, eating in the kitchen is not as widespread in Italy as it is in many other countries—the kitchen still retains its primary and historical function as the room where meals are prepared and served. Modern urban kitchens are superbly equipped and have been designed to be as efficient and practical as possible, which includes making sure that every gadget has a place where it can be stored out of sight. Hygiene is also a major concern, and the work surfaces, wall tiles, and floors are all guaranteed to be sparkling clean.

In a country house, where there is more space, it is possible to create a more relaxed and cozy atmosphere, where friends can stand talking to the cook while the meal is prepared. In this type of farmhouse kitchen it is not unusual to find a table and chairs for informal eating, and the room will be arranged to make a happy fusion of practicality and pleasure. Gaily colored tiles may decorate the walls; pottery and majolica will be on display alongside collections of treasured copper pots and pans; and woven baskets, rush table mats, and trays all help to add a rustic touch to the room. Usually, when guests arrive, the table will have been set with a brightly woven linen cloth, pottery plates, and simple glasses, ready for the meal.

Italians love large gatherings and delight in producing huge quantities of delicious food for any number of people. The one piece of furniture every family seems to own is a table large enough to seat at least 10, and preferably 20, family and friends. Whether it is in the kitchen or dining room, this table represents the heart of Italian hospitality. It is the place where everyone gathers to share news and gossip, to discuss future plans, or simply to enjoy the pleasure of each other's company, mingled with the comforts of lovingly cooked food and plentiful amounts of wine. The table hums with the noisy exchange of views, and diners often change places during the meal, so that they can talk to someone else. All around the table, children tumble around in a way that would give a Victorian nanny palpitations, but which parents, grandparents, and assorted aunts and uncles regard with indulgence.

Lunch often lasts the entire afternoon, as dish after dish is brought out to sighs of appreciation. A meal usually starts with a simple *antipasto*, such as *crostini* spread with chicken livers, pesto, or tomatoes, smoked meats, or sausages. There is then a pause before the steaming bowls of aromatic risotto or pasta appear. Nothing is

PREVIOUS PAGES This converted farmhouse kitchen cleverly combines essential modern conveniences with a traditional scheme. In the middle of the room, the antique French wooden campaign table provides space for preparing meals and eating informal lunches, and folds away when not required. The open fireplace in the corner is used in winter for roasting meat on a spit in classic Umbrian style, while more conventional types of cooking are done in the oven or on the hob. Pots, pans, ceramics, and cooking utensils are all arranged conveniently at hand, in a way that is both decorative and practical. The warm, friendly atmosphere of the kitchen is conjured up by the combination of pretty tiles and the bright ocher colorwash on the walls.

OPPOSITE The imposing 15th-century dining room at the Torre di Bellosguardo is decorated with colorful frescoes in the vaulted ceiling, following a tradition handed down from the ancient Romans. The richness of the ceiling makes a strong contrast with the plain white walls and the dark wood of the massive doors.

A black fire screen and the chandelier, hung on an intricately worked chain, are traditional wrought-iron work. Above the carved relief of the magnificent fireplace, the arms of the Michelozzi family proclaim the owners of the tower. The small stone niche in the corner of the room, with its carved stone surround, is for washing.

The center of the room is dominated by a massive carved wooden table, which after years of careful polishing has developed a rich patina that would be impossible to reproduce artificially.

hurried; there is plenty of time for another long break before the next course—a huge platter of meat. The same leisurely pace continues through the remaining courses of vegetables, salad, fruit, cheese, or dessert.

This passionate enjoyment of food repays the time and care spent in its preparation. Cooks make sure that they buy the freshest ingredients from the nearest outdoor market, where colorful fruit and vegetables grown locally are piled high in tempting profusion, next to stands selling creamy Italian cheeses, cured meat and sausages, and crusty breads, cakes, and cookies.

When the dinner is a formal one, then great care is taken with the presentation of both the table and the food. There is a long tradition of beautiful glass coming from Venice, where it has been made for centuries in factories on the nearby island of Murano. Although Venetian glassware has been widely copied, some of the finest pieces are still made there. Wine glasses have exquisitely thin bowls supported on intriguingly shaped stems that may be decorated from the inside with *latticino*: fine white lines that spiral upward. They are the perfect vessels from which to drink the best wines Italy has to offer.

White linen tablecloths and napkins are often cherished heirlooms that are proudly passed on from one generation to the next. Even today, a girl getting married may be presented with a trousseau of linen for the table and bedroom, sewn or collected by her mother and grandmother, or embroidered by nuns who have been working on it since the day she was born. Given this antecedence, it is no wonder that it is painstakingly laundered to look crisp and perfect.

Delicately decorated porcelain may also be inherited; if not, traditional designs—from plain white, through floral patterns, to brilliantly colored contemporary ceramics—are still in production from long-standing centers all over Italy, such as Este Ceramiche e Porcellane and Richard-Ginori. Add to this a whole array of glistening silver knives, forks, spoons, and candlesticks, set off with a wonderful flower arrangement, and you have a truly glamorous setting for a glittering dinner.

When the tables are not laid, Italian dining rooms tend to look quite sparse, with just a few important pieces of furniture giving a strong visual impact. Refectory-style tables with heavy carved legs are popular, and are often placed in the center of the room, surrounded by chairs. A sideboard or serving tables, and sometimes a capacious cabinet for storing all the china and glass, are often the only other pieces in the room, but the style of the furniture and décor vary according to region and city.

OPPOSITE At night this dining room in a Venetian *palazzo* sparkles with light reflected from the candles in the Murano glass chandelier onto the walls and the lustrous terrazzo floor, an effect that is heightened by the Venetian mirror hung on the far wall. The gilded console table below the glass is contemporary, inspired by Venetian furniture designs, yet greatly simplified. An 18th-century antique leather-embossed screen stands in the corner of the room, while the wall beside it is dominated by a painting of *The Rape of Europa*. A circular Venetian walnut table, with matching chairs, provides a convivial setting for an intimate dinner.

OVERLEAF LEFT This carved sideboard stands at one end of the room used for dining in Villa Saraceno. A pair of decorative French candlesticks has been carefully placed on top of it, so that they stand on each side of a portrait of a cardinal, a composition of stark simplicity that contrasts with the white walls and dark wooden furniture.

OVERLEAF RIGHT The dining room of this former hunting lodge is cleverly arranged and decorated to look like a Dutch still life. The beautiful inlaid lute leans against a leather-covered book, while other volumes prop up a grand silver platter decorated with grapes and pomegranates. In the foreground lies an 18th-century wooden flute and Indian gunpowder containers that are made from shells and glow with a pearly luster. The reflection of the window can be seen on the side of the clear glass vase and together with the spray of roses further enhance the Old Master illusion.

Below this still life, and adding to its effect, a Venetian silver tureen standing on a carved wooden chest is flanked by an antique silver carafe and urn. Brown leather-covered chairs, with their characteristically shaped backs, surround the heavy wooden table and emphasize the room's masculine qualities.

THIS PAGE AND OPPOSITE A pair of beautiful old wooden doors frame the way through to the dining table beyond (left). All the characteristic features of an Italian rural house—the white walls, the exposed beams, the terracotta floor, and the dark wood furniture—are on show in this room. Just inside the door, a large antique cupboard holds the household's plates and glasses on its deep shelves.

Outside the dining room, at the bottom of the stairs, is a tall wooden washstand (right), which is now used as a decorative piece of furniture.

OVERLEAF LEFT Solid elm planks form this robust 18th-century rustic table, which is typical of Umbrian country style. Sitting on it is an old Sicilian terracotta pot. Behind the table, the huge *pietra sirena* fireplace makes the room cozy in winter and is often used for open-fire cooking. Within the hearth is a large hook, traditionally used to hang a pot of beans, a classic Umbrian staple food. Above the doorway, a 19th-century Russian-painted tin tray is a surprising decoration in this otherwise very Umbrian kitchen.

OVERLEAF RIGHT This room was converted from a rustic building that once housed pigs. The color on its walls was carefully copied from the original sty and is animated by a set of prints that depict regional peasants' costumes. The painted table is large enough to sit 14 guests.

THIS PAGE AND OPPOSITE This Tuscan rustic cupboard (left) is large enough to hold all the family glass and china. It is painted both to protect the soft wood and to give the piece a touch of elegance. Simple white pottery and plates wait for the table to be set (below). The style is extremely pure and unpretentious, as close as the owners can achieve to the timeless simplicity of Italian rural living.

OVERLEAF Ceramic tableware is produced all over Italy, with designs varying from region to region. Many Italians like to collect a range of pottery, both old and new, which can be both decorative and functional. The simplest designs are just spattered drops of color contrasting with a pure white ground. Circular patterns are formed by turning the piece on the wheel as a loaded brush gently deposits a ring of color. Folk motifs of flowers, leaves, and birds are popular, while the more sophisticated designs from Deruta are based on the arabesque motif seen frequently in renaissance decoration.

The big saucepans used daily for boiling pasta are hidden out of sight in cupboards, but cherished copper pots, pans, kettles, and pudding molds, carefully handed down through generations, hang as decoration from the roof beams or above the sink. Typically found in Italian country kitchens, they add color and warmth to the dark wood and the white walls.

Traditional and modern cooking methods live side by side in this kitchen (opposite)—the open fire is ready waiting to be lit for roasting meat on a spit. Color and pattern are added to the kitchen by small-patterned tiles, and a line of glass pots, arranged by size, that contain everything from pasta to herbs.

The shallow stone sink on this page is of a kind frequently found in Tuscany and Umbria.

The wooden plate rack above this stone sink provides a time-honored way to drain the clean dishes (above). The dishes, pots, and pans are not only close at hand, but also add color and interest to this corner of the room. Beside the plate rack, stacked high in an alcove, is a collection of egg boxes waiting to be packed with the brown speckled eggs from hens that have been scratching around in the sunshine.

On the other side of the same room (opposite), a bench seat has been made to fit over what was once the cattle feeding trough, while rustic chairs can be added for more seating. A floor covered with reclaimed heavy stone slabs, stone walls that have been left unrendered, and roughly hewn beams still recognizable as trees, all help to emphasize the country feel of this kitchen.

TRANQUILLITÀ

PREVIOUS PAGES LEFT A swirling arabesque of leaves and flowers, in a design that has its roots in antiquity, separates the dado from the upper part of the wall.

PREVIOUS PAGES RIGHT Light fills this Venetian bedroom and illuminates the 18th-century wall paintings of gentle country scenes. Below the molding, festooned swags of fabric create a border, while the dado, which is painted to look like stylized marble, is grained in pink over a pale terracotta ground, adding richness and balance to the pictorial decoration above. In contrast to the richness of the wall decoration, the low stool in front of the fireplace is loosely draped with a green cloth, and the bed is similarly covered with creamy silk.

OPPOSITE Dominating the room in which it stands, this magnificently carved bed displays a grandeur entirely befitting its setting. The four posts and headboard carry the mattress high above the polished terracotta floor, so the bed is the same height as the writing table at its foot. Behind it a *trompe-l'oeil* fresco of a shell-topped niche seems to make the bed even more imposing. The same arched theme is repeated over the doorway in a lunette where the figure of Apollo languishes in verdant countryside. The room is suffused with warm light reflected from the cantaloupe colorwashed walls, which enhances the lavish decoration and makes a calm contrast with the traditional white linen on the bed.

A PERFECT BEDROOM IS A PLACE OF REPOSE. A tranquil refuge from the world, where the senses are lulled into a spirit of relaxation at the end of a busy day. A room where the colors of the decoration and the arrangement of the furniture conspire to create an ambience in which to rest and to dream.

The heat of the summer accounts for much of the look of Italian bedrooms, especially in country houses where the walls are thick and the windows small. All through the day, the shutters are kept closed, so that the room can remain shady and cool. These rural bedrooms can seem rather dark and somber to those used to living in more northerly climes, where sunshine and light are to be rejoiced in rather than repelled. During the winter, the thick walls and the small windows keep heat loss to a minimum, but this means that the rooms appear even darker.

Larger, grander houses have correspondingly bigger windows and more ceiling height in the bedrooms, which aids airiness. Here, too, it is usual to have shutters instead of curtains hanging at the windows, and similarly the custom is to keep them closed during the day. What air there is circulates through the louvers.

The most important piece of furniture in an Italian bedroom is the bed itself, the *letto matrimoniale*. There are many different kinds of beds; styles vary from region to region and with the importance of the house—beds made for noble families share an imposing grandeur whatever their provenance.

Characteristic are the beds with tall headboards upholstered in rich silk. They have extravagantly baroque shapes, their curved edges rising in a series of flourishes to their lofty tops, a design that complements the pattern in the damask silk. The bedspread is generally made from a matching fabric. In the grandest rooms, a set of bed hangings may fall from an elaborate corona above, generating a sense of theater in the room.

Carved wooden beds are also typically Italian. Some beds merely have an intricate headboard, while others have four beautifully carved corner posts that support the bed high off the ground. It is unusual for Italian beds to have the canopy normally associated with a four-poster. The wood may be a natural dark color, or it may be painted and gilded.

One form of bed seen all over Italy is the *baldacchino* or tester. Made from iron, it is simpler in form than French versions and has straight, tall posts in each corner and linking crossbars at the top. These may be left plain or hung with voile, cotton, or lace to form curtains that can be tied back at the corners.

Many Italian beds are made from wrought iron, and the curves formed by the blacksmith create a huge variety of designs for head- and footboards. Normally the metal is left black, but sometimes it is painted white, which creates a lighter effect in the bedroom.

Simplest of all are the beds with plain wooden headboards found in rural Italy. Many of these previously belonged to tenant farmers and are now back again in the bedrooms of restored rural houses, where they naturally look entirely appropriate.

Most Italian bedlinen is white—pure white sheets in the finest cotton with a seductively silky feel, or soft luxurious linen. Although starching and ironing these sheets and pillowcases is time-consuming, Italians seem to feel that an immaculate and inviting bed is a necessity rather than a luxury. Bedspreads are also usually white and may be made from heirloom lace, crisp pique, painstakingly embroidered cotton, or drawn threadwork. Most beds have both pillows and a long, hard bolster on which to rest your head, but the latter can feel very uncomfortable to the unwary.

Bedroom floors, like floors in the rest of the house, are usually made from terracotta or terrazzo, although wood and marble floors are also found. Carpet is very rare, but rugs may be used sparingly to add a splash of pattern and color to the room.

Since the time of the ancient Romans, the Italians have been perfecting the art of bathing, and today their bathrooms are often both practical and luxurious. Many people start the day with a quick, invigorating shower, but most also have the option of a bath when they need to relax. Italians pay great attention to the bathroom furniture, so that everything from the sink to the faucets, is beautifully designed. Soaps, pumice stones, loofahs, and sponges are likely to be natural and of the best quality, as will the bottles of botanical oils—such as lavender, rose, and jasmine—or scented salts that are kept on a shelf or in a cupboard. After bathing, Italians love to wrap themselves in thick, white towels or fluffy bathrobes made from the finest Egyptian cotton, which is beautifully soft and absorbent. Linen, lace-edged facecloths and hand towels are also put out on towel rails and, although they look too pristine to be touched, they are used every day.

Bathroom floors have to be made of a material that will not be damaged by water, and terracotta or ceramic tiles are a popular choice. Occasionally floors are done in mosaic, which can be very effective, particularly if the design has a watery theme. The finest bathrooms have marble floors, walls, and washbasin surrounds, but usually glazed tiles are found around sinks to protect walls from splashing. They can be plain white, or in one or more of the thousands of different patterns that are produced in Italy, especially in Sicily. Some of the tiles have raised borders, which can give the wall surface a three-dimensional effect.

All the expected ingredients of a rural bedroom are here: the low beamed ceiling, the small chestnut-framed window, the white walls, and the traditional high iron beds. Not quite a matching pair, the bedsteads enhance the room with their different profiles of swirling metal, and the pretty green covers introduce some color.

Curtains are rare in Italian bedrooms, their place being taken by wooden shutters, which shade the room on sunny afternoons, and help to retain the heat during the winter.

OPPOSITE A contrast in dark and light, the pale
terrazzo floor, the creamy bedlinen and the stark
white walls create a harmony of opposites in this
serene bedroom. The luxury of the sumptuous
French Aubusson tapestry hanging high on the
wall is offset by the simple beds and lack of clutter.
Mosquito nets provide a reminder that practicality
can have its own elegance.

THIS PAGE The scale of this simple bedroom in a
villa designed by Andrea Palladio gives it grandeur.
The very high arched ceiling enhances its noble
proportions and confers a surprising importance
on the plain wooden furniture. The French country
lit bateau is made up with crisply laundered linen.
Behind it, the table is just large enough to hold a
book, and a lamp with a stand made from an
old church candlestick. Other furniture in the room
includes a Venetian 19th-century rush-seated
chair, painted dark green with gilded outlines.
An antique woven rug, in dusty pink and grayish
blue, introduces texture and pattern to this
otherwise austere bedroom.

OPPOSITE A very rare example of an original set of bedhangings and decorations survives in this bedroom in Villa Bianchi-Bandinelli near Siena. The walls and the bed are covered in a white linen cloth printed with *chinoiserie* designs derived from Jean Baptiste Pillement, which was brought from Paris in the late 18th century. Below this, the dado is painted to look like marble, and this almost plain expanse of color gives weight and contrast to the decoration. The furniture has been painted with motifs copied from the fabric by local artists in colors that would originally have been the same, but have since yellowed.
In the center of the room a magnificently carved and gilded bed once provided rest for a pope, whose coat of arms has been emblazoned on the headboard as a memento of the occasion.

THIS PAGE The extravagant shape of this contemporary headboard echoes the style of the 18th-century example opposite. The thick Fortuny cotton used to upholster it is printed with a traditional large-scale damask design of stylized leaves and flowers.

ABOVE This 18th-century wall painting is framed by elegant arabesques of stylized acanthus leaves, birds, and flowers. The dresser is covered with antique damask and displays contemporary Venetian glass, made to old designs.

OPPOSITE The dramatic decoration in this bedroom owes much to 19th-century stage design. In the foreground, painted curtains are opening to reveal an enchanted Italian landscape of fanciful

medieval castles, lakes, and hills. The excitement of theatrical perspective is emphasized by the painted lambrequin above, hung with huge tassels and topped with *trompe-l'oeil* decorations painted in grisaille to look like intricately carved stone. At the corners of the room, pillars appear to support the heavy molding and the painted beams of the ceiling. The *letto matrimoniale* is covered by a white bedspread that dates from the 1920s and is edged with thick crocheted borders.

The 19th-century fresco decoration in this pretty bedroom (opposite) was rediscovered under a coat of plaster and carefully restored to its present faded charm. What remains has a subtle delicacy of color and tone. The Italian instinct for balance is shown in the placing of the pair of white-painted iron beds so that their intriguingly shaped tops echo the border above. Bold yellow stripes in the fabric covering the headboard and foot panel add a splash of stronger contrast, while the fully blown roses and lilac flowers pick up the tones found in the wall behind.

A glimpse into the room through the door shows the same fabric hung at the windows (this page). The brilliant yellow is picked up in the two majolica plates displayed on the marble-topped chest of drawers.

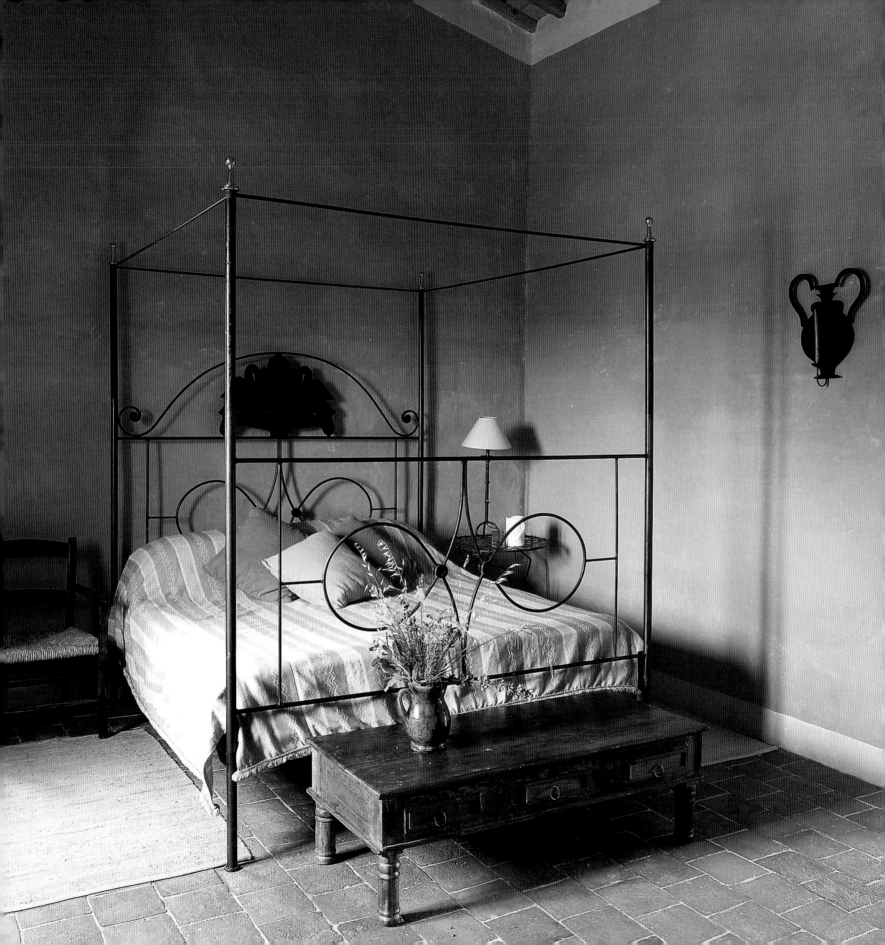

OPPOSITE A contemporary version of the traditional iron bed dominates this country bedroom in Umbria. The graceful curves of the design at its base and head provide a contrast with the structure of the upright four posts. The walls have been colorwashed with warm terracotta, giving the room a welcoming air. At the foot of the bed a low table complements the other furniture in the room.

THIS PAGE A battered old wood plank door opens into this cozy country bedroom. Rough plaster walls with just a hint of earthy color combine with the simple furniture—the wooden bed, the stool, and the chest—to make a room of rustic simplicity. Its unpretentious charm is enhanced by the old ceiling beams and the traditional terracotta tiling on the floors.

THIS PAGE AND OPPOSITE A shallow old stone sink (above) rescued from a dilapidated farmhouse kitchen has been reinstated upstairs to make a basin of the utmost simplicity. The luxurious bathtub (right), which is sunk deep into the floor, owes more than a passing reference to ancient Rome, with its pale gray mosaic tiles and water trickling slowly from the aged brass spout. The natural color of the walls creates a warm atmosphere in which to relax and revive.

OVERLEAF Simple in the extreme, this round stone bowl has been restored and is now used as a washbasin with old-fashioned faucets and an ancient cupboard above. Peeping from behind its curtain, it looks as if it has always been there, but is in fact part of a long and sensitive restoration of a Tuscan farmhouse.

LEFT Sicilian tiles are renowned for their numerous designs and brilliant colors. They have been arranged around the washbasin to provide a decorative focus for this pretty Tuscan bathroom (above). The sweeping curve that defines the shower area (below) is an imaginative diversion. It emphasizes the contrast between the pure white of the ceiling and floor, and the soft pink of the walls.

THIS PAGE Here, the Sicilian 19th-century hand-painted tiles that adorn the end of the bathtub and the splashback protection for the shell-shaped washbasin are decorated with a three-dimensional pattern in purple and blue. The palest blue in the tiles is repeated in the wall behind. This house was not built with a bathroom, so a bedroom has been converted, giving the luxury of space for a large, open shower.

AL FRESCO

*Terraces, Courtyards,
and Garden Rooms*

IN THE SUMMER much of Italian life is lived outside. When the air is warm, there is nothing more natural than enjoying a glass of wine with friends beneath a vine-covered arbor, or sitting in the cool shadows of the *loggia*. In country gardens the trees provide shade for long lunches, or a quiet place to relax and take a siesta.

In cities, towns, and villages, restaurants spill onto the sidewalk, cordoning off areas in front of their premises with shrubs and flowers in pots. During the day, large umbrellas or awnings shelter diners from the blazing sun. Later on the town's finest buildings are floodlit to provide diners with a magical backdrop.

In the early evening the streets and squares erupt into a bustle of activity as people wander up and down the main street in the daily *passeggiata*, which is as much a part of Italian life as a plate of pasta. Children play noisily, while adults greet each other like long-lost friends, even though it was only yesterday that they last met. The activity gradually subsides as everybody goes home to dinner.

A yard is a rare treat in a town or city, but there are often balconies festooned with trailing geraniums; and at the top of many buildings, old and new, there are minuscule terraces formed between tiny roof spaces. Some of the older villagers prefer to sit in chairs outside their front doors, however, so they can keep a beady eye on local events.

Walking along narrow Italian streets you can sometimes glimpse a private courtyard through an open door. These tiny oases might have a small patch of grass, flowers, and plants, a stone bench, and wisteria, roses, or vines climbing up the walls. Courtyards are far more numerous than you might expect, for most are hidden behind building façades, and are secluded havens for the people who live there to enjoy.

In the fine villas of Lombardy, Tuscany, and the Veneto, and those around Rome, the garden has a graciousness and formality that complements the architectural distinction of the house and surrounds it with a setting in harmony with its style. In these "Italianate gardens," tall cypress trees line the driveway leading up to the villa, and neatly clipped box hedges are laid out symmetrically in complex shapes around flowerbeds and paths. Garden architectural features—such as sweeping flights of stairs, cascading fountains, balustraded walls, stone plinths, and obelisks—are important features that are placed in balanced equilibrium like mirror images. Classical statues animate the garden and are sometimes complemented by an outdoor theater, formed by curving box hedges and fronted by a grass apron stage for the performance of drama or music. These gardens are best enjoyed in the cool of the evening, when the sun casts long, dark shadows over the lawns,

PREVIOUS PAGES Villa Cetinale was designed in 1680 by the great baroque architect Carlo Fontana for the Chigi family, important bankers and patrons of the arts. The cream façade (left) is punctuated by tall arches, within which an open *loggia* provides a cool space where plants grow in profusion, their bright green leaves thrown into contrast by the white walls and finely carved marble busts supported on sculpted plinths (right).

A gravel path that runs from the gate to the entrance is lined on both sides by topiarian box hedging. This formalizes and delineates the structure of the garden in a manner similar to the way the stone quoins and rose brick detailing define the architectural features of the house. This emphasis on proportion and symmetry is enhanced by the positioning of important statues by Giuseppe Mazzuoli and lemon trees in terracotta pots on each side of the path.

Beyond the villa and its carefully constructed gardens, the hills rise sharply, creating a backdrop of oak trees that underlines the relationship of Cetinale with the surrounding landscape.

OPPOSITE Spaciousness and light characterize the lofty *loggia* at the Torre di Bellosguardo. The glazing in the arches overlooking the courtyard means that this is a warm place to sit all the year round, and that tender plants, which would not flourish outside, grow happily.

OPPOSITE A feeling of relaxation pervades this shady haven in the hills of Chianti. Positioned under a mulberry tree, the rustic bench and table are the perfect places to enjoy a glass of wine among the trailing passion flowers, aromatic mint, and vines. The grand curling leaves of the acanthus are a constant reminder that this plant has inspired artists and architects since the days of ancient Rome.

OVERLEAF LEFT The *barchessa* was added to Palladio's Villa Saraceno in the 19th century, linking the main house to the farm buildings. Now it provides a place for large numbers of guests to eat *al fresco*, looking out through the columns to the walled garden beyond. Above the heavy beamed ceiling, the grain storage area has been converted into extra bedrooms.

OVERLEAF RIGHT Framed by heavily fragrant jasmine flowers, this outdoor dining room, sheltered from the sun by a tiled roof, overlooks a pretty courtyard filled with climbing roses and pots of geraniums and petunias. The fireplace on the back wall can be used for roasting meat. A collection of baskets and flagons adds to the rustic feel of the *loggia*.

and the colors are thrown into high relief, or in the early morning when the air is fresh with a pinkish haze in the sky, and the scent of the plants is enhanced by the dew.

Around farmhouses and less architecturally important buildings, the yard has a more informal aspect. The planting is more natural and, in contrast to the classical Italianate garden, where there are very few flowers, it is much more colorful, with roses, lavender, irises, lilies, and many other plants growing in profusion, not in carefully delineated flowerbeds but springing up from the grass or forming the boundary with the fields beyond. The trees that are scattered about these yards are sometimes a relic from the days when they were still working farms, and figs, plums, peaches, and pears were seasonal produce. Gnarled old olive trees are often kept more for their decorative look than for the purpose of harvesting the olives. They are an ever-present reminder of the past history of the building and a felicitous fusion today of the yard and garden with the surrounding countryside.

In the country, a garden is a natural adjunct of the house, and the shady space created by the open-sided *loggia* is the link between the two. Sometimes the *loggia* is an architecturally splendid affair, which acts as the main entrance into the house (see page 54), while on other occasions it is a simple garden room in which to sit with family and friends and enjoy a meal or a glass of wine. Another popular spot in many Italian gardens is the swimming pool, and here the shade may be provided by a canvas umbrella or awning big enough to cover a table for a long, lazy lunch.

Houses along Italy's mountainous coast, where the rugged cliffs dip precipitously into the sea, have pockets of land that have been turned into tiny gardens. What they lack in space they make up for in color—masses of pots, tumbling with purple and carmine bougainvillea, abundantly flowering pink and red geraniums, blue plumbago, orange nasturtiums, and white jasmine have as their backdrop the dazzling azure sea. And there is just enough room on the terrace for a table and a few chairs, or a couple of sunbeds on which to lie back and absorb the view.

Living outside demands furniture that is comfortable and light enough to move around. In its most basic form, a hammock strung between two trees is fine for one person to while away the time, idly reading a book. If there is a group of people to seat, then prettily shaped metal chairs are a popular choice, because they can withstand the odd thunderstorm, but they are too hard to sit on for long periods. More comfortable and relaxing are cane or canvas chairs, which are often grouped around a low table under the trees or on the terrace.

THIS PAGE AND OPPOSITE Nearly at the top of the Torre di Bellosguardo, the open terrace overlooks its garden and the countryside around Florence. From its high vantage point, the magnificent view, which you can enjoy over breakfast or a leisurely read, proclaims the original purpose of the 12th-century tower as a lookout, giving early warning of hostile bands of strangers. Lower down the building, thick fortified walls provided protection for the original medieval occupants at a time when this part of Italy was overrun with battles and feuds.

OVERLEAF Long, warm days are the perfect time to eat and entertain *al fresco*, surrounded by scented flowers and stunning views. Formal gardens, with their artfully constructed *parterres* of box, intricate paths, and statuary, demand to be explored and admired, while country gardens encourage relaxation in the shade of a tree or some other enticing spot. Windowboxes and pots overflow with geraniums and petunias, and in early summer roses flower in gardens and hedges, tumbling over walls and arbors.

OPPOSITE Deep in the heart of the countryside, this is a garden that is almost completely natural, filled with wildflowers and grasses. Walking from the house to the rustic stone table means brushing through clumps of sweet smelling lavender and bushes of rosemary. It is a perfect vantage point from which to admire the beauty of the surrounding hills. Shaded in the spring, by summer the tree affords little protection from the scorching rays of the midday sun. But if you wait until nightfall, you can lean against the warm stones of the stable wall and watch the fireflies dance beneath a starlit sky.

BELOW This secluded arbor in an Umbrian country garden provides a tranquil setting to sit and drink coffee in the shade and listen to the wind as it rustles through the silver-gray leaves of the old olive trees. In the background, the view across the hazy hills is framed by a border of roses.

OVERLEAF Pink petals float on the crystal surface of this azure pool, blown from the surrounding roses and peonies. Relaxing on a chaise longue beneath the awning, idly eating peaches and cherries, must surely rank as one of the more sybaritic pleasures Italy has to offer.

FURTHER READING

Harold Acton, *Tuscan Villas*, Thames and Hudson, New York, 1984.

Sophie Bajard and Raffaelo Bencini, *Villas and Gardens of Tuscany*, Terrail, Paris, 1993.

Leonardo Castellucci, *Living in Tuscany*, Abbeville Press, New York, 1992.

Paul Duncan, *Traditional Houses of Rural Italy*, Abbeville Press, New York, 1993.

Joe Friedman and Marella Caracciolo, *Inside Rome*, Phaidon, London, 1993.

Christopher Hibbert, *The Grand Tour*, Putnam, New York, 1969.

Christopher Hibbert, *The Rise and Fall of the House of Medici*, Morrow Quill Paperbacks, New York, 1980.

Christopher Hibbert, *Florence, The Biography of a City*, W. W. Norton & Co., New York, 1993.

Edmund Howard, *Italia, The Art of Living Italian Style*, St. Martin's Press, New York, 1997.

Ian Jenkins and Kim Sloan, *Vases and Volcanoes*, British Museum Press, London, 1996.

Jane Martineau and Charles Hope (eds), *The Genius of Venice*, Royal Academy Exhibition Catalogue, H. N. Abrams, New York, 1984.

Georgina Masson, *Italian Gardens*, H. N. Abrams, New York, 1961.

Anna Mazzanti, *The Art of Florence*, Scala, Florence, 1997.

James Morris, *Venice*, Faber and Faber, London, 1960.

Jan Morris, *The Venetian Empire*, Harcourt Brace Jovanovic, New York, 1980.

H.V. Morton, *A Traveller in Italy*, Dodd, Mead, New York, 1982.

Michelangelo Muraro and Paolo Marton, *Venetian Villas*, Rizzoli, New York, 1986.

Laura Raison (ed.), *Tuscany, an Anthology*, Facts on File, New York, 1984.

Alex Ramsay and Helena Attlee, *Italian Gardens*, Robertson McCarta, London 1989.

Paolo Rinaldi, *Tuscany Interiors*, Benedikt Taschen Verlag GmbH, Cologne, 1998.

Giandomenico Romanelli, *Palladio*, Giunti Gruppo Editoriale, Florence, 1986.

Vivian Russell, *Edith Wharton's Italian Gardens*, Bulfinch Press, Boston, 1998.

Catherine Sabino and Guy Bouchet, *The Essence of Italian Country*, C. N. Potter, New York, 1995.

Catherine Sabino, *Italian Country Living*, Thames and Hudson, London, 1988.

Ronald Shaw-Kennedy, *Venice Rediscovered*, Art Alliance Press, Philadelphia, 1978.

Francesco Venturi and Elizabeth Helman-Minchilli, *Private Rome*, Rizzoli, New York, 1998.

Frédéric Vitoux, *Venice, The Art of Living*, Stewart, Tabori and Chang, New York, 1991.

Alvise Zorzi, *Venice: The Golden Age 697–1797*, Abbeville Press, New York, 1983.

INDEX

AUTHOR'S ACKNOWLEDGMENTS

In writing this book I was fortunate in having two editors: Caroline Bugler, who provided the original inspiration and impetus, and Slaney Begley, whose lively enthusiasm ensured its successful completion. The fact that it looks so good is due to the creativity of the book designer, Anne Wilson, and to Simon Upton, the photographer, whose skillful eye selected and composed the superb pictures. We were supported by Anne Fraser and Sue Gladstone, and I would like to thank them all for making the production of this book such a happy experience.

In Italy, the owners of the many wonderful houses that make up the book generously allowed us to photograph their interiors, and I am particularly grateful to Contessa Shirley Carraccilo, Conte Andrea Bianchi-Bandinelli, Anita Broggi, Tony Walford, Conte Antonio Bolza, Lord Lambton and Claire Ward, Frédéric Bouilleux, Senora Trois, The Landmark Trust, my elegant hostess and friend in Venice, the kind friends who own a beautiful hunting lodge in central Italy, and the others who prefer to remain anonymous.

I would like to say thank you also to some of the other people who helped me in my research and gave me introductions to interesting houses. Maria Fairweather was a kind hostess in the Villa Wolkonsky in Rome and has been generous in her advice and encouragement. Catherine Fairweather has been an imaginative source of ideas, Harry Scio was welcoming at the Poste Vecchia, Sarah Townsend at Palazzo Terranova, and Marcello Salom and Giovanni Giurlani in Lucca, and Contessa Jane Da Mosto in Venice.

At Ornamenta I have been enormously supported by Alexa Turnbull, Melanie Taylor, Sally Crawford, and Laura de Haan, and I am very grateful for their patience and help as the book progressed.

VISITING ITALY

Some of the houses and gardens that are featured in this book may be visited by appointment.

Villa Bianchi-Bandinelli, Geggiano, Siena

Villa Cetinale (garden only), Cetinale, Sovicille, 53018 Siena

The Ridotto, Casino Venier, San Marco 4939, Venice

The Torre di Bellosguardo is a hotel and can be visited year round at Via Roti Michelozzi No. 2, 50124 Florence. Villa Saraceno is available for private hire through the Landmark Trust, Shottesbrooke, Maidenhead, Berkshire SL6 3SW, England, tel: (01144) 1628 825925. Details of all 166 of the Landmark Trust's properties are available in the *Landmark Handbook*, price £9.50 including post and packing, refundable against the first booking. Other quality properties in Italy can be hired through CV Travel, 43 Cadogan Street, London SW3 2PR, England, tel: (01144) 171 591 2800; Simply Travel, 598–608 Chiswick High Road, London W4 5RT, England, tel: (01144) 181 995 8277; and International Chapter, 47–51 St John's Wood High Street, London NW8 7NJ, England, tel: (01144) 171 722 0722.

PUBLISHER'S ACKNOWLEDGMENTS

The Publishers would like to thank Katherine Morgan at AD/Italy for her assistance, the staff at Lupus Travel Ltd for their help and patience, and J.D. Lee for the index.

PHOTOGRAPHIC ACKNOWLEDGMENTS

(FLL=Frances Lincoln Limited)
All photographs copyright © Simon Upton, except for those on the following pages: 18–19 Private Collection; 20 Joe Cornish; 29 Chris Caldicott; 44–5 background Christopher Drake © FLL; 45 top right *Rubelli* at Percheron, London; 45 bottom left Christopher Drake © FLL; 70–71 Simon Upton © AD/Italy; 98–9 Christopher Drake © FLL; 106–7 Simon Upton © AD/Italy; 108–9 Simon Upton © *The World of Interiors*; 111 Simon Upton © Country Life Picture Library; 130–31 Simon Upton © *The World of Interiors*; 142–3 Christopher Drake © FLL

Project Editor Caroline Bugler   *Editor* Slaney Begley
Editorial Assistants Tom Armstrong and Tom Windross
Production Stephen Stuart
Editorial Director Kathryn Cave   *Art Director* Caroline Hillier